The Ultimate Holiday Club Guide

Alan Charter
and John Hardwick

The Bible Reading Fellowship

OPENING THE BIBLE

Dedications

This book is dedicated to my late father, 'Digger' Brian Charter, whose God-given love for children drew me to faith and was inspirational for my life. He is missed and loved more than ever.
Alan Charter

And to my parents, Leslie and Ruth Hardwick, who since long before I was born have been involved in reaching out to children, in everything from beach missions to ongoing children's clubs. They have helped me to see the importance of reaching children who know nothing of the Bible or of God's love for them.
John Hardwick

Acknowledgments

The authors wish to thank the following people for all their help and inspiration: Alan's wife Claire and John's wife Rachel, Sue Doggett, Jackie Lambert, Barbara Lilley, Joanne Robinson, Jane Towers, Paul Wilmott; and past members of the Saltmine Children's Team: Sue France, Marie Moore, Joe Fisher, Mel Owen and Mich Ellwood.
The following are works of the authors listed below and are used with their permission: 'Sid and Basher' adventure story: Joe Fisher; 'Commitment' sketch: Joe Fisher and John Hardwick; 'Count the Cost' sketch: Rachel Munoz Hardwick.
With many thanks to Linda Hills for the sheet music in Appendix B.

Cover credits

The photograph on the back cover shows the Saltmine Children's Team (1992/93) in action. Pictured from front to back and left to right are: Mel Owen as Melly the Clown, John Hardwick as Yoyo, Mich Ellwood, Alan Charter and Bert and Lucy.

Foreword

Both Alan and John worked with me as part of the Saltmine Team project. I wish I could say that I taught them all they know... but this book would immediately prove me wrong!

I do know, however, that they are both young men of integrity, creativity and warmth. What they write has been forged on that toughest of all anvils—experience! They have a heart to reach out to children and their families, and the skills to do that capably and professionally.

I am glad to commend this distillation of their combined years of experience. I believe that it will be a positive contribution to the task of kingdom building in and around your church. So use it, and let your imagination run riot for the King!

Stuart Pascall, Saltmine Trust
November 1995

Contents

An Introduction

*W*henever I think of holiday clubs, they stir up all sorts of memories in my mind. They have become an integral part of my life—probably because I have been a part of them all my life. I grew up with them and soon found that they had grown on me. Throughout my childhood I was both on the receiving and the giving end of our local holiday club, Diamond Diggers. Praise God they are still digging today! The Bible is the diamond mine, full of precious 'gems', and all the leaders become 'diggers'. My memories are a jumble of excitement, touching stories (told by Digger Dave), laughter at all the drama and the puppets—but, most of all, a real sense of love from people who wanted me to be there. It was just a couple of months before my seventh birthday that I responded to that love and made the choice for myself: to ask Jesus to come in and give a new direction to my life. That was the simple start of faith, which slowly began to grow—and continues to grow today.

This book is intended to be like a cookery manual—covering all the essential cookery skills, but with the added advantage of including the ingredients, too. It is divided into two halves. Part One is simply a guide to help you set about planning and putting on your holiday club. It looks at all the different aspects of planning, ranging from the framework of decisions that need to be made early on in the planning to the methods of communication which work best with the age group—and how you can use them. There are a number of general guidelines relevant to working with children, and a few handy hints to help you get the most out of your programme. Part Two gives you three ready-to-use teaching outlines. You can pick the one that appeals most to you, or run the complete programme over the next three years.

Each theme has been born out of the principles laid down in Part One of the book. You may find it useful to refer to both parts of the book as you read through, to see how the ideas are put into practice. All the material comes from the involvement of John and myself in children's ministry—both the experience and the lessons learnt. Each theme has been thoroughly field-tested. Please feel free to pick and mix the material, and use and adapt it to your needs.

We hope that there will be something here for everyone. Whether you are on the starting blocks wondering which way to go, or looking for fresh new ideas after several years' experience; whether you want to run a large holiday club, or are looking for material to suit a small weekly club, The Ultimate Holiday Club Guide is designed with you in mind.

Alan Charter
October 1995

PART ONE

Why? A Biblical Perspective

Over the past few years there have been a growing number of books written on the increasingly popular subject of working with children, and rightly so. For too many years the whole area of children's ministry has been neglected. It should not be a passing phase that loses impetus, for the Bible suggests that children are very much on God's heart. I'm sure we are all too aware of Jesus' challenging statement that 'whoever does not receive the Kingdom of God like a child will never enter it.' Children should not just be viewed as the 'church of tomorrow', for, although they will be the church of tomorrow, they are very much a part of the church of today. Therefore we should actively seek to welcome children into the *family* of God. We need to consider the importance, or lack of it, that the local church places on children's work and examine our own approach and response to what the Bible teaches.

A bit of history

When the children of Israel were delivered from Egypt, God instructed Moses to institute the Passover. One of the instructions he gave regarding the Passover was, 'In the future, when your son asks what this observance means, you will answer him, ''By using great power the Lord brought us out of Egypt, the place where we were slaves. When the king of Egypt was stubborn and refused to let us go, the Lord killed every firstborn male in the land of Egypt, both human and animal. That is why we sacrifice every firstborn male animal to the Lord, but buy back our firstborn sons. This observance will be a reminder, like something tied on our hands or on our foreheads; it will remind us that the Lord brought us out of Egypt by his great power.'' ' (Exodus 13:14–16).

Much later on when the children of Israel crossed over into the Promised Land, Joshua was commanded to erect a pile of stones. God instructed him, 'These stones will remind the people of what the Lord has done. In the future, when your children ask what these stones mean to you, you will tell them that the water of the Jordan stopped flowing when the Lord's Covenant Box crossed the river. These stones will always remind the people of Israel what has happened here' (Joshua 4:6–7).

The Bible points us to the traditions of the Jewish nation to remind their children constantly of the things God had done for their race. They show the principle, reinforced throughout the Old Testament, of handing down God's law from one generation to another. 'He instructed our ancestors to teach his laws to their children, so that the next generation might learn them and in turn should tell their children' (Psalm 78:5–6).

Solomon's wise words from Proverbs 22:6, 'Teach children how they should live, and they will remember it all their lives', form a solid foundation. He stresses the importance of education, using scriptural guidelines, from a formative age. This enables children to grasp a knowledge of the truth, so that it will remain with them and form a foundation for the rest of their lives.

Children we can learn from

In the Bible there are a number of occasions when God has chosen to work through children and young people; for example:

Joseph was a young man of about seventeen when God started to reveal plans of how his life would take shape through prophetic dreams (Genesis 37–50).

Samuel was a young boy when he was called by God, in a way that most of us rarely experience. God spoke to him and gave him a very important message (1 Samuel 1–3).

David, the shepherd boy who trusted God, killed Goliath and put to shame the older doubting members of Saul's army! (1 Samuel 17).

Jeremiah was assigned by God to be a prophet before he was born and called at a young age to speak out for God (Jeremiah 1).

The boy and his lunch at the feeding of the 5,000. It was a young lad who faithfully gave all that he had to Jesus: a simple, uncomplicated, trusting action (John 6:1–15).

Recognizing our responsibility

There is a tremendous ignorance in this country about the simple fundamental principles of the Christian gospel. The vast majority of people only have a vague idea what Christianity is all about. Bible knowledge is almost non-existent. On television quiz shows the occasional biblical question is hardly ever answered correctly. First and foremost, the Christian family has a responsibility to teach their own children the word of God. But this responsibility doesn't end with our own families. The Church recognizes its responsibility to teach the Christian message to successive generations.

We are commanded to teach our children the word of God so that they will know what the Bible teaches about God's plan for their lives—eternally. Salvation is the work of the Holy Spirit, but we have a command to preach and to instruct so that the Holy Spirit has a foundation on which to work in people's lives.

A society which is deprived totally of any knowledge of the Bible becomes a society which is a seed-bed of anarchy. If we produce a generation of children who know nothing about the word of God we are producing a generation which is going to be dishonest, greedy, violent and law-breaking. What a tragedy to produce a whole generation of children who have never heard the story of the crossing of the Red Sea or David and Goliath, or who know nothing about the person of Jesus, of the parables he taught and the miracles he performed; or the wonders of the Church's birth as recorded in Acts.

Often, there is a void between what the Church offers to children and what children want from the Church. We need to create an atmosphere where we see the real value of children; the value that Jesus put on children. We need to create an atmosphere in our churches where children feel happy and at home. Sometimes the actual impression made on a child is more important than what they remember of the things they are taught. If a child goes into church and finds it a dull place, a repressive place where they have to be seen and not heard and where they are not really wanted, they will grow up with a totally false idea of what church is about. It may be a perception close to what a church is, but it is certainly not what a church ought to be. We need to create an atmosphere in church where children will feel they are coming into a happy, welcoming place. A place where they can be themselves and where there is a God and a saviour who really wants to welcome them.

Where to Start?

Initial planning

Holiday clubs do provide a wonderful opportunity to reach many children who would otherwise never hear about the God who loves them. In fact it is estimated that only 14 per cent of children in the UK have *any* contact at all with church. Much of that contact itself is fairly superficial and it still leaves a whopping 86 per cent without any knowledge of Jesus. That provides us with a constant challenge to meet the responsibilities of evangelism.

Holiday clubs are one such means of meeting that challenge and sowing spiritual seeds into hearts of children who otherwise wouldn't hear. Holiday clubs should never be seen as simply a means by which flagging churches can give a 'quick fix' to their Sunday schools, trying to boost numbers in the short term. They can, however, draw together a wide variety of individuals from the church, or inter-church, family for a concentrated focus of evangelism. This won't just fall into place. The pointers on the pages that follow are designed to guide your thoughts and discussions as you plan.

First of all, you need to establish amongst the leadership where the holiday club fits into the overall outreach programme of the church. This means long-term planning; clubs are not just a stop-gap to fill the black hole of the summer holidays. You need to ask:

- *Is your church welcoming to children?*
- *Are their needs actively provided for?*
- *Could your church cope with a sudden influx of children?*
- *How does your church handle the balance between its ministry to the adult congregation and its ministry to youth and children?*
- *Could the existing structure be improved by making a few minor changes?*

Once these questions are satisfied and a consensus to continue with the planning is reached, you will arrive at the first stage of a rather big adventure for the months that follow. Welcome!

Before taking the next step and engaging fully in your preparations, you'll need to give careful consideration to the following points:

- *WHO are you aiming at?*

Will you be inviting children in the 5–11 age range, or just be concentrating on the infant or junior end? Do you have sufficient people and facilities to cater for the under-fives? Even if you're not intending to advertise your club for the under-fives, there may still be a need to provide a crèche for the children of leaders or helpers. Will there be teenagers present? If so, how will you cater for them? Are you planning a special event/programme for them? Will you involve them in the club?

How widely will you be advertising the club? Are you aiming at mainly church family children or are you wanting to reach children in your local schools? If you are aiming at the latter, what are you going to do to enable children to bridge the gap between school and church?

● *WHAT are you aiming to achieve?*

Think about the end results before you start! Do you want to build foundations for an ongoing relationship with the children who attend the club? Would your current children's programme be able to accommodate them? Will your resources cope with another five, ten, twenty, or fifty children?

Are you planning just to teach, or are you going to give the children an opportunity to respond to the gospel? How do you plan to nurture the children who respond to the gospel message? Do you have the facilities and manpower to follow up their response?

Here are some aims you could adopt:

Aims for running a holiday club

● *To build up relationships between the church and the local community.*

● *To bring children into a caring and loving environment where they feel valued and where relationships matter.*

● *To present Christian teaching in a relevant way through the activities, and to reflect it in team relationships.*

● *To encourage the development of social skills and moral values.*

● *To provide interesting, stimulating and creative activities for children outside the school environment.*

● *To offer the opportunity and experience to develop new skills and discover new interests.*

● *To let children discover positive ways of having fun!*

● *To introduce children to the wider-age-related programme of the church.*

These are some fairly fundamental issues that are good to address at the outset. They set the framework for the preparation that follows. The conclusions you reach will differ according to your situation. You'll find some of the issues covered in the preparation section, enabling you to think through the stages involved.

By now you will have realized that this is no single-handed job. You will need a committed core of people to share responsibilities, support each other and surround the holiday club in prayer. From here on in you'll be working together to get the wheels in motion.

Preparation

These next few pages cover a number of practical stages in the preparation. At the end you will find a useful checklist to help you to keep track of your schedule.

Premises/Venue

A good one to tackle at the outset: it is essential to find the right place to house your holiday club. You may be fortunate enough to have suitable and sizeable church buildings you can use. Often, though, they do not prove very child-friendly, nor do they give you the greatest level of flexibility, especially if there is fixed furniture such as pews, pulpits and pillars. Give consideration to play areas. Your church or hall may be suitable for any stage-based presentations but you'll also need room for a variety of games to take place.

Check out other local venues. School halls often give the space and flexibility required. These may need to be booked well in advance, so be prepared. The cost will usually need to include a caretaker on site during the club.

Another option is to hire a marquee. This won't be the cheapest option and you will, of course, need somewhere to put it. However it does provide you with a wonderfully different atmosphere—especially for that 'Big Top' feel (see Theme 2). It is advisable to have a security team who are prepared to sleep in the marquee. You could be in for a bit of a let down otherwise!

Money/Budget

Another one to deal with early on, and a worthwhile reason to maintain a good relationship with your church treasurer! There are a number of specific costs to be met, mainly:

Premises—hire charges, heating and lighting etc.

Publicity—printing costs and any artistic input.

People—gifts and expenses to any invited evangelists.

Resources—necessities for crafts, equipment for sports.

Photocopying—funsheets, notices, leaders' guides, etc.

Prizes—optional take-home reminders for the children.

Snacks—bulk purchase of squash and biscuits!

Decoration—transforming your venue into a place the children really want to be in.

Staging—do you have it? Do you need it? Do you plan to hire it?

These are some of the areas you may need to budget for. You may have others, so make sure they go in the budget too.

Timing

Choose carefully when you plan to have your holiday club. Which school holiday best suits you and the children you are planning to invite? If you are planning to hold the club at the beginning of a school holiday, you have easier contact from the end of the term to when you begin. At the other end, however, you can put children straight into any regular programme you run. Is the time slot you are planning for the club likely to clash with anything else? A school holiday trip, another church's club, or a local authority scheme? *Check it out before you book it up.*

It may be that an after-school holiday club is better for you—run in the evenings. Or you might want to do just a one-day 'spectacular'. Whatever your plan, check it out and book it in. It is worth bearing in mind that under the current conditions of the Children's Act, as long as the holiday club meets for less than six days in any one year no registration with your local authority is required. If under-8s are present, however, the local authority must be informed in advance of the nature of the activity which is planned. You'll find their number in your local telephone directory.

Training

Your leaders and helpers will find any training you can provide for them invaluable. If you are inviting a professional person or team to come and help run your club, enquire as to whether they would be available to give some training in advance. At the very least, you should bring all your leaders and helpers together to run through the aims of the week and where the limits of their responsibilities lie. Remember, if you don't make people aware of what you expect of them, then they won't live up to your expectations.

Teaching programme

The teaching programme will form the heart of your holiday club. It is worth spending time thinking through your programme to make sure it's at the right level for the children you intend to reach. We have devoted the next section, entitled 'What to do', to the finer points of how to put a programme together; the aim being to enable you to fit your own ideas into a usable format. You may prefer, though, to start with one of the three field-tested, ready-to-use themes from the second half of the book!

What you present to the children will remain with them for a long time. It is therefore important to strive to do the best for them. If you feel that there is no one suitable to lead the stage-based teaching, it would be worthwhile considering using professional people. There are some suggestions of people you could contact given in the 'Which Resources?' appendix on page 145.

Publicity

If you don't tell your local children about your holiday club, then they won't be there! Obvious, I agree, but nevertheless true! There are a number of options that you can choose from. You may be happy simply to rely on word of mouth through your Sunday school, junior church or local schools. Posters, though, will reinforce the message and remind the reader. These could be done by a local printer, or you may have artistic talent in your congregation you can draw upon. Alternatively, why not set the challenge before your existing children's groups to put some material together in their own style!

Providing your budget allows, perhaps the best method is to print colourful fliers which can be put into the hands of each child to take home. If you are stuck for ideas, try CPO (their details are on page 145). They have a range of colourful fliers, posters and other advertising materials ready to overprint with your details.

One of the best advertisements of all, if you have the people available, might be to approach your local schools and offer to take an assembly. Schools are usually happy to encourage the church's involvement, and you can give the children a taste of what is to come. Remember, though, with the wrong approach you can do more harm than good, so make sure you are fully prepared before you set foot into the school!

Finally, nearer the time it is worth contacting the local press and making them aware of your plans.

Roles to share

We'll look at this in more depth at the end of this section. However, it is important to speak to individuals and delegate the appropriate tasks early on. Holiday clubs do provide a great opportunity to draw together a wide variety of the church body who might welcome the opportunity to work together.

Evaluation

It is good to keep track of developments as you go along. Make sure that you are on target with all the preparation in the run up to the holiday club. If, for whatever reason, things aren't quite working to plan, be prepared to adjust your programme accordingly. Encourage feedback after the holiday club to help shape your plans for next year!

Prayer

Prayer is the key to any holiday club. Bring everything to our wonderful heavenly Father in prayer and let him be the one to worry about the problems. 'Do not be anxious about anything, but in everything by prayer and petition, with thanksgiving, present your requests to God' (Philippians 4:6).

Roles and responsibilities

Holiday clubs provide a wonderful opportunity for everyone in the church, from teenagers to the oldest members to get involved in some way. Here is a suggested outline of the type of areas that need people to oversee:

● **Registration co-ordinator.** *This job would suit an efficient, organized person with some spare time. Registration can either be done in the weeks running up to the club, or on the day. If you want the children to register in advance, you will need to make a clear request on the publicity material for parents to contact you to register their children. If you prefer the children to register on the day, bear in mind that you'll need a team of helpers to cope with the frantic onslaught on Day One. Whether you choose to pre-register or to register on the day, it is advisable to take details of each child's name, address, date of birth, age, phone number and any necessary medical details (such as asthma or allergies). You will need to split groups into age bands, and possibly sub-section them into teams. It is advisable to issue each child with a colour-coded card/sticker/badge to identify them and their team. Have a 'welcome' team available at least 15 minutes before the start to make the children feel at home.*

● **Team leader.** *Team leaders need to have a high level of responsibility. They will be allocated to a particular team or age band, depending on how you split your group. They will need to stay with their group the whole time, sitting with them during the stage-based sections and leading them through the various activities in the rotation times. Team leaders have a wonderful opportunity to befriend and encourage their teams, but also need to maintain a level of control too. They will have the best opportunity to get to know the children really well.*

● **Team helpers.** *Team helpers are needed to support their team leaders and to stay with the teams at all times. They are the ones who will be free to fetch anything the team might need, during games for example, and to take younger children to the toilet when the need arises.*

Activity Leaders

● **Games** *If possible, a sporty person should be the one to put together and lead the games for the groups during rotation time. It is best to*

base the games in a fixed location, each group coming to that area when it is their turn to play games.

● **Craft** *Someone will be needed to organize a simple craft each day, related to the overall theme, and where possible tailored to the daily themes. Again, it is best to allocate a fixed location for the crafts, which the children rotate to when it is their group's turn to do the craft activity.*

● **Funsheets** *Someone is needed to design an age-related sheet that reinforces each day's teaching. Ready-to-use funsheets are in each of the themes in this book. The children take their funsheets home each day.*

● **Activity helpers** *Activity helpers are spread between the different activities, giving specific support where needed.*

● **Time keeper** *Although sometimes useful to prompt the stage team, this person has to be alert during the rotation time as a point of contact between the groups and to ensure everyone knows where to go during rotation time. He or she would also be responsible for ensuring the children have all relevant reminders and notices at the end of each day, informing them of the events which are planned over the course of the club.*

● **Snack team** *Most children's favourite team! You will need to have copious supplies of squash and biscuits on hand. Groups can take their refreshment between the activities, whilst they are partaking in a snack and chat time, or working on their funsheets.*

● **First aider** *The first aider is essential—do not overlook the importance of this role. If there is no one available who holds a current certificate, get someone trained now. If all else fails, try contacting your local St John Ambulance.*

● **Disciplers** *Disciplers need to have a good understanding of the children attending the club. When presenting children with the gospel, you must be prepared for their response. Discipling or counselling primarily involves listening and being open to the Holy Spirit's prompting. Do NOT put words into a child's mouth, or hurry them to a point of commitment. Instead, allow them the time they need and let them respond naturally to the gospel message. Ideally, disciplers should be local people who will be able to see the child again and keep in regular contact.*

● **Publicity** *A pre-event role! This person will need to organize any posters, leaflets and fliers etc., keep in touch with local schools and, if* possible, arrange some 'taster' assemblies. The publicity co-ordinator is also the point of contact with the local press. The press might be able to send someone along to give your club coverage, or you could send them a photograph with a covering press release.

● **Floaters** Always useful! Floaters are people who can only commit themselves to occasional days or sessions. It is handy to have people who can see where the gaps and shortfalls are and slot in accordingly, or provide cover for another team member who has to drop out for any reason.

● **Stage team** Finally, you do need to have a team of people who are capable of presenting the teaching material from the front. There may be people in your church who are capable of doing this, or you may prefer to bring in a professional evangelist or stage team. Book early if you are intending to use professional people. Find out what they can offer you and let them know the theme you are planning for your club. Suggestions of professional people to contact are given in the 'Which Resources?' appendix on page 145.

CHECKLIST

Dates arranged . . . . ❑

Venue booked . . . . ❑

Budget set . . . . ❑

Teaching programme chosen . . . ❑

Publicity arranged . . . . ❑

Schools contacted . . . . ❑

Stage team booked (if necessary) . . ❑

Training planned . . . . ❑

Staging available . . . . ❑

Local authority contacted . . . . ❑

Snack team . . . . ❑

First aid . . . . ❑

Disciplers . . . . ❑

Publicity co-ordinator . . . . . . ❑

Floaters . . . . ❑

Stage team (own) . . . . ❑

Prayer co-ordinator . . . . ❑

Stage designer . . . . ❑

Venue decoration team . . . . . ❑

Musicians . . . . ❑

Roles to fill:

Registration . . . . ❑

Team leaders . . . . ❑

Team helpers . . . . ❑

Games leader . . . . ❑

Craft leader . . . . ❑

Funsheet co-ordinator . . . . . . ❑

Activity helpers . . . . ❑

Time keeper . . . . ❑

Items to purchase:

Craft materials . . . . ❑

Games equipment . . . . ❑

Pens for funsheets . . . . ❑

Sweets . . . . ❑

Prizes . . . . ❑

Squash and biscuits . . . . ❑

Evaluation carried out . . . . . . ❑

What To Do!

Use this section as a reference guide to help you plan your stage-based teaching programme.

 ### Using the Bible

When two people both tell the same story, one will have their audience rivetted, whilst the other will leave their audience confused. Why? Because story-telling is an art form and when mastered will have the audience on the edge of their seats, hanging on to every word.

From ancient times, stories have been a means of communication; carried from town to town, from person to person and handed down through successive generations.

Storytelling focuses the children's attention on the person telling the story. If you use visual aids their attention will be split between the visual aid and the storyteller. When you have only yourself as their visual aid their attention will be on you alone. You will be the means by which they use their own imaginations. You will be the vehicle for their point of identification with a character from the story you are telling.

The Bible is a wonderful source of stories. There are hundreds of them, varying from love stories to stories of battle, murder and assassination. From stories of kings to stories of ordinary people caught up in dramatic situations. Stories that cover the whole of a person's life, or stories that just cover one incident in a person's life (and that is all you hear of them).

Jesus was one of the greatest storytellers of all time. The stories he told can be related to children time and time again without losing their freshness.

Don't use biblical stories just to illustrate a particular moral point. Although many of the Bible stories do have moral lessons, they have a far greater value than just the moral point alone. Don't just concentrate on well-known stories, but try to use less familiar ones too.

For example, the story of Esther teaches us that God is able to work his plan through events and situations which might, on the face of it, look totally hopeless. Through the courage of his people he is able to turn bad to good and bring about the downfall of those who oppose him. The story of Esther also teaches us to keep our loyalty to God whilst living in a secular society.

Storytelling does, of course have its disadvantages. There is a greater degree of responsibility on the person telling the story. There is an art to keeping children's attention whilst presenting the story, and knowing how to regain it if they get distracted! Once you have mastered the art of storytelling you will soon find that you are your own best visual aid!

Here are some useful guidelines when preparing a Bible story:

1. Read the story right through several times! An obvious, but essential first step! If the story you want to tell occurs in more than one place in the Bible, read all the different accounts.

2. Use your imagination. . . without altering the story.
Imagine, for example, what it was like for Zacchaeus:

a) Zacchaeus was unpopular because he was a tax collector.

b) He was lonely. What is it like to be lonely and have no friends apart from a few who do the same job as yourself?

c) How would it feel to be shorter than everyone else? Always trying to look over other people's shoulders?

d) Point out how strange it would be to see a rich man like Zacchaeus, a tax collector (compare him with a civil servant), climbing a tree, hoping no one will see him. But when Jesus picks him out everyone sees him!

All these things help in telling this story.

3. Be careful not to Westernize. Although stories need to be told in a way that children can understand, make sure you retain their Eastern background. Familiarize yourself with the facts surrounding the story in its original biblical setting.

4. Don't be too gruesome. Old Testament stories are often very gruesome, but don't, for example, dwell too much on the story of Jael driving the tent peg through Sisera's head with a mallet as this would upset many children. However, although it is not appropriate to focus on the violent aspect of a particular story, neither should you leave out all the gruesome, violent stories, because this would present a lop-sided view of the Bible.

5. Be prepared to read the story over and over again until it makes a deep impression on you and you have grasped its meaning for yourself.

Technique

1. Everyone has their own technique for telling stories. One person can keep children's attention very well by hardly moving at all while another person will act out a great deal of the story. The important thing is to do what you are most comfortable with and to develop your own technique. If you have prepared sufficiently, you will have enough material to keep their attention.

2. Avoid leaving the application right to the very end. Try not to tell a story and then spending the last five or ten minutes trying to apply the story. The children will listen while you are telling the story and then switch off! Try to weave the application right through the story, perhaps breaking off from the story at a very exciting point so that the children's attention is still focused on you, applying it in some way and then coming back to the story.

3. Don't try to stretch the lesson too far. It suffices to plant the Word of God and let the Holy Spirit do the rest.

4. Allow the spiritual lessons to sink into your own life. You'll then be equipped to communicate them to others. Remember that it is impossible to teach anyone something which you have not first learnt yourself, and it is impossible to excite others if you are not first excited yourself.

5. Read through the story picking out the main points. Think about the lessons that are illustrated by the story. Which points do you want to bring out?

6. Work out how you are going to approach the story: for instance, setting the scene can be done in many different ways:

● *You may ask the children to close their eyes and imagine the scene.*

● *You may choose to start halfway through at an exciting part of the story and then recap what has happened before (for example, Jonah got stuck in the belly of a big fish! What was he doing there?)*

● *You may choose to start with the children's own experience: 'Have you ever had a day when . . . ?'*

Try to apply the lesson right through the story. For example, tell the story of Jonah up to where God calls Jonah to go to Nineveh, but Jonah goes in the opposite direction. Lesson: Do we always do as we are told? Do we always do as God tells us? Story continues. . .

You may choose to tell a story as a straight narration, or from the point of view of one of the characters, or in some other way. And remember. . .

- *Be lively*
- *Be clear*
- *Be confident*

Introductions and endings

Think of an introduction and an ending.

Take, for example, the story of Naboth's vineyard in 1 Kings 21. Introduce it by explaining that there was a king in the Bible who had a huge and beautiful garden.

1. One day, while admiring his own garden, the king looked over the wall and saw Naboth's vineyard. He wanted it.

2. He went to see Naboth. 'I've noticed your small vineyard, I'd like to own it! So how much will it cost?' Naboth was amazed to have the king at his front door! 'I'm sorry, King, it's not for sale; you see my father owned it before me and his father before him, it's been in my family for generations! So it's not for sale. Sorry!'

3. The king went home and sulked! (I wonder if we sometimes sulk when we don't get what we want.)

4. Queen Jezebel, who was a very wicked lady, said 'What's up with you?' King Ahab told her all about it, but she just laughed at him. 'You're the king aren't you? So you can have whatever you like; I'll get the vineyard for you.'

5. She went and got people to tell lies about Naboth. This caused the people to get so angry that they came and took him away. That was the end of Naboth.

6. Jezebel went to see the king. 'Oh husband dear, guess what? The vineyard is yours!' The king was so happy.

7. But God was angry and said, 'Because you have done such a terrible thing I'll get rid of you both in the same way you got rid of Naboth'.

8. Then the king was sorry for what he had done. But he still had to accept God's punishment.

9. God hates it when strong powerful people pick on weak people who are not so strong. We need to be satisfied with the things we have and not constantly wanting more.

The End.

Examples

Samuel

Introduction—Is there anyone here who lives in a tent? Is there anyone here who has ever been in a tent? Well there was a boy in the Bible who lived in a tent, not a small tent but a huge tent used to worship God in. Just him and an old priest called Eli.

Ending—This time God didn't give his message to Eli the priest but to Samuel the young boy. You see it doesn't matter how old you are, God thinks you are special.

Zacchaeus (Luke 19)

Introduction—There was a man in the Bible who had loads of money, loads 'n' loads of money! A lot of people think that if you've got lots of money, you'll have lots of friends—but that's not necessarily true. This man didn't have many friends—in fact, he was quite lonely. He had a job that no one else would do. He collected money (taxes) for the Romans—the enemy. He was only small, so just imagine him collecting the money. . .

Ending—No one else had time for Zacchaeus because he was a cheat and a traitor. But Jesus had time for him, and after Zacchaeus spent some time with Jesus he changed for the better. Jesus thinks that we are important and he has time for us; it doesn't matter what we may or may not have done. We are all special.

The Philippian jailer (Acts 16:16-34)

Introduction—Have you ever had one of those days when everything seems to go WRONG? When it happens to me I moan and become very grumpy. Well, Paul and Silas were having a day when everything had seemed to go wrong. They had been beaten and thrown into jail. . .

Ending—Although everything had seemed to go wrong, it had turned out to be a great day, a day to remember. God doesn't necessarily work in the way we expect him to.

Daniel:

Introduction—Is there anyone here with a long or a strange name? Well, there was a guy in the Bible who had a long *and* a strange name. His name was Nebuchadnezzar and because he was the most powerful king in the whole world. . .

Ending—Despite the very difficult life Daniel had, he remained faithful to God, right through from when he was a young man taken from his home as a slave until he was a very old man.

Remember: In the introduction you need to set the scene. Try to think of a way which will get the audience's attention straight away. In the ending, sum the story up in a few short sentences. Don't drag it out with lots of points—your audience will switch off!

Memory Verses

Memory verses are a very effective way of helping children to remember biblical truths that hopefully will remain with them as they grow up.

When choosing a memory verse it is a good idea to use a modern translation that the children can understand. The Good News Bible is the most easily understood, whereas the NIV or NRSV are more word-for-word translations.

The best way to help children learn a memory verse is to be as imaginative as possible in the way you present it. Try different methods such as:

- music
- a drum beat
- learn the sign language for the verse
- make up actions
- balloons—putting a word on each balloon and pop them as they learn it, etc.

Using visual techniques

Drama

Drama can be used with any age group. Keep the drama short and simple, bearing in mind that children have a short attention span. Drama and mime can be used effectively to reinforce a teaching point. In an age where children spend so much time passively before the television, it is important to encourage active participation.

When preparing and writing a drama sketch its worth remembering the following points:

1. The audience. Put yourselves in the shoes of those who will be watching. Think about the things that will interest your audience and build them into the sketch.

2. What do you want to communicate to your audience? If you aren't sure what the main point of your sketch is, the audience won't be either!

3. Are the characters ones the children will be familiar with?

4. Is the drama suitable for the occasion? Is it in good taste or might it embarrass or offend?

Drama workshop icebreakers

1. Sit in a circle. Each person in turn stands up and says their name followed by a noise or action or both. The rest of the circle then stands up and repeats what the first person said and did.

2. The old faithful 'Heads, shoulders, knees and toes' always gets a laugh!

3. 'My Bonnie lies over the ocean.' Stand in a circle facing inwards with right arm and leg inside the circle. Sing through the song and each time a word beginning with B is sung, switch from right to left arm and leg.

4. As people parade around the room the leader gives them instructions to follow.

a) Walk cheerfully

b) Walk sadly

c) Walk like a very old person

d) Brush your teeth

e) Chew some very sticky toffee

5. Mirrors: Get everyone into pairs. One person has to wash and brush their teeth and comb their hair and the other person has to pretend to be their mirror image.

6. Interviews: choose two people, one to be the interviewer and the other their guest on a chat show. The rest of the group then suggest who the interviewer might be and who the guest might be and also the topic for discussion.

7. Bible stories: form groups of about four or five. Choose a Bible story for them to act out. Then choose the style in which they are to act it. For example, in the style of a western, a whodunit or a soap. Give 15–20 minutes for each group to work out their sketch and then have them perform the result (if they want to!).

8. Human Pyramids (not for the faint-hearted!): form groups of between four and ten. Give the groups one minute to arrange themselves in whatever shape you tell them. For example, a saucepan, or a cube, or for added entertainment value, a rhombus!

9. What is it? In a circle pass around an object; each person has to think of a different use for it (for instance, a saucepan could be a hat or a tennis racket).

10. Situation Game: Joe was walking down the street when he saw a woman at the bus stop he thought he knew. He crept up behind her, put his hands over her eyes and to his horror. . . Split people into groups who have to decide what happened next and act it out.

11. Nursery Rhymes: recite a nursery rhyme in the following styles:

a) like a five-year-old

b) like a person with no teeth

c) like a Shakespearian actor

d) like a policeman

e) like someone with a cold

It might be fun to try them with different accents too!

12. Advertising: form groups of between four and six and give each a made-up product to advertise. If you are really hi-tech, get someone to video their presentation and show them back to the whole group during a 'commercial' break!

Mime

Mime can be used with any age group. It is another good way to capture the attention of the audience—you'll be amazed how quiet it is whilst they're watching and concentrating on the mime! Most of the audience try to work out the message behind the mime for themselves. It is very visual and crosses language/age/culture barriers. Also, mime is very simple—don't feel that you have to be a budding Marcel Marceau before you contemplate taking part in mime!

You can mime to a piece of music, a song or a poem. You can mime out a Bible story and bring out the main point of the story. You need very few props for a mime.

It's good to use make-up for mime, which is especially useful for bigger audiences, because it projects the face. It is also helpful when you perform in front of people you know, as it sets you apart—they'll see a mime artist rather than you and hopefully take what you're doing more seriously. The make-up also hides any blushes! For that final touch you could also wear white gloves.

Here is a very simple mime face:

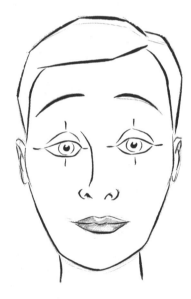

There are examples of mimes in the three themes in Part 2.

Clowning

Clowning is a very colourful, lively and funny way to communicate with children (and adults). Because clowns are so unique and bright they keep the attention of children and portray characters the children can relate to. Clowns can learn lessons and at the same time teach them to their audience. We have found that clowns play a very valuable part in work with children and they always seem enthralled by them. However, it is worth being aware that the under-fives have to be handled with a little more care as they can be frightened and feel threatened by clowns.

Sketches without meaning serve little purpose. Decide on the point of your clowning sketch and the teaching that you are wanting to draw out. The meaning behind the sketch could be a moral one, such as sharing with each other or working together. (Examples of sketches to use can be found in the Big Top theme in Part 2.)

How do you start?

The first thing to do is to decide on your character. What kind of clown are you going to be? This will influence how you dress. For example, working with a partner, you could choose to make one clown generally daft, but be an older clown who has learnt a lot of tricks. The other clown could be a learner clown who is quite often shy and not very self-confident, but very eager to learn. The second clown should therefore look a bit younger, lack the experience of the older clown and possibly wear an L-plate as part of the costume.

Make-up is important. You can use stage make-up or ordinary face paints, but make sure that, whichever you choose, it is easily removable. We have found baby wipes ideal for removing make-up. Practise your facial expressions in front of the mirror, because conveying emotion is important. Don't use too much make-up, this only makes it harder and more painful to remove.

The next thing to do is to decide on a name and stick to it. Use a catchy, but fairly superficial name that even the youngest member of your audience can catch on to.

Becoming a clown will involve learning some new skills! There are a variety of skills to choose from, although juggling is quite essential.

Skills

1. Magic colouring book:

This is no ordinary magic colouring book! They are a little hard to come by but can be found in, or ordered from, juggling shops. They come with instructions and are simple and effective to use.

2. Diabolo:

The diabolo is an apple-core shaped object which is balanced and spun on a piece of string tied to two sticks. It can be tossed into the air and over the arms and legs and is especially good to use out of doors.

3. Stunt stick:

Commonly known as a devil stick, the stunt stick is not too expensive an item to add to your collection of skills. You need good coordination to use it.

4. Unicycling:

Only for the very agile and committed! This is a hard skill to learn and will involve a few bruises. However, once you get the hang of it, it looks spectacular. The smaller the wheel the easier to ride, or so you'll be led to believe! Certainly, the wider the wheel the easier! Juggling shops will give you the names of suppliers.

5. Juggling:

Finally the basic essential skill: the rudiments of three-ball juggling are roughly as follows:

● *Step 1—Throw one ball from one hand to the other trying to keep a consistent height in your throwing. The path of the ball should be from side to side. The ball should not be thrown forwards.*

● *Step 2—Have a ball in each hand. If you are right-handed start with the ball in your right hand. Throw it to the left hand as in Step 1, but this time just before it lands in your left hand throw the second ball into the right hand. It is a staggered action, so do not release the balls at the same time. Both balls should be thrown to the same height. Do not pass one across the bottom.*

● *Step 3—Having mastered two-ball juggling, the fun starts! Hold two juggling balls in your right hand. This is the sequence: The first ball leaves the right hand and the second ball is thrown from the left to the right hand and before it lands the third ball is thrown from right to left. It's best not to think too hard about it! It is actually quite simple.*

Once you have mastered three-ball juggling you have a wide choice of juggling props. You can use PVC professional juggling balls/bags, or there are solid plastic coloured balls, luminous balls, balls that will bounce when you drop them, hoops, apples, oranges and for the very brave—eggs! There are other options like flaming torches and knives but they are not advisable for children's events!

For a simple trick try juggling with two balls in one hand and holding a third and making it follow one of the balls as it goes up and down. Slightly harder is the overhand grab when you snatch the ball from above instead of letting it fall into your hand. If you are already a juggler there are books that will show you more advanced techniques and there are also some computer programmes that teach you how to juggle. A figure on the screen actually juggles; there are also written instructions and the chance to slow the juggling balls down in mid-flight!

Juggling is a marvellous way to illustrate a talk. For example, you could illustrate who is in control of our lives: is it us, other people or God? Are our lives going the way we want or are we out of control? God has a purpose for our life and when we become a Christian he is in control. That doesn't mean we won't have our ups and downs (!) but he has promised to be with us. Whose hands are you in?

For a simpler illustration you could use three different coloured balls with three different faces drawn on them to illustrate how we're all different and special.

Puppets

Puppetry is a very visual and entertaining way to deliver an educational message or sketch. Puppets have enormous scope when it comes to communicating clearly and effectively. They appeal to all ages whether used within a full and varied programme or as a simple one-off. They can be used to initiate or reinforce a teaching point through their portrait of a real-life situations. Children readily identify with them and everybody listens when puppets speak.

Anybody can be a puppeteer with a bit of practice. After a while you will be able to make the puppet speak, move realistically, even show emotions—bringing them to life. Practice is the key word. Use a mirror to help you visualize the puppets' movements and perfect their life-likeness. Try using the different emotions to reinforce what you are saying. (For even more ideas, try watching or getting hold of a video of 'Sesame Street', and see just how life-like those characters are!)

Knowing what to say with your puppets also develops with practice. Script writing may not seem easy, but it is probably not as hard as you think. Use everyday situations that your audience may be familiar with, or adapt a Bible story to a script that you can use. Always keep your audience in mind. Something that works with one age group won't necessarily work with a different one.

Writing your own scripts

Points to remember:

Keep it simple, usually the simpler the better.

Pick one specific point to communicate.

Keep it short—remember that your arms will get tired!

Make sure what you say is relevant to the audience you have.

Use lots of short speeches to create as much interaction between the puppets as possible.

Don't over-spiritualize the puppets' characters; keep them down to earth!

Don't be afraid to take existing material and adapt it to suit your personal situation.

How to perform

Puppets can be used in a variety of ways, either on their own, or with the operator. Firstly, they can 'speak' in one of three ways:

1. The puppets can interact with each other, with the operator(s) hidden inside a puppet theatre.

2. The puppet can pretends to talk to the operator (e.g. whispering in the operator's ear).

3. The operator can use ventriloquism to provide the voice of the puppet.

Once you have got comfortable with whichever method you choose to use, then take note of these practical guidelines:

Make sure that the puppets are clearly visible.

Learn your script whenever possible.

Choose a name and character style for your puppet and stick to it.

Use puppets that are appropriate for the size of your audience. e.g. A small glove puppet is not very visible for a large audience, so use a 'muppet' style puppet that works better with bigger groups.

Types of puppet

There are many different types, styles and sizes of puppet. They range from fairly basic to very complex. Some puppets can be used on their own; others need to be used with a puppet theatre or screen. This enables the operator to be out of sight and gives the puppets a good

backdrop and framework, creating more of an impact.

● *Muppet style—usually just an upper body, sometimes with legs, sometimes with with strings or sticks attached to give the arms greater movement. Their large heads and mouths make them good for audiences of any size, but they are particularly impressive with larger groups. They work best in a puppet theatre.*

● *Glove puppets—made famous by Ed the Duck and Sooty, these vary from elaborate felt and fur designs to a simple decorated glove or paper bag.*

● *Sock puppets—a simpler version of the above made from. . . you guessed it!*

● *Finger puppets—made with narrow tubes of material or card, with any variety of decorations. Usually come in 'family' groups, and definitely not for large audiences.*

● *Marionettes/string puppets—fairly complex. Harder to make and generally take more practice to master.*

● *Rod puppets—usually simple cardboard cut-out characters, stuck on a stick. They are rigid in their movements and need a screen, but are very easy to make.*

● *Shadow puppets—similar to the above, but using a sheet for a screen and strong lighting to give a new dimension.*

You could try making your own puppets with the children. With a bit of imagination (something children have in plentiful supply) there is a wide variety of things you could use to make your puppets. So keep your eyes open and get gluing!

Helpful hints

Finally a few tips for using the large muppet style puppets—from those experts Bert and Lucy. . .

Dos & Don'ts

General

Do *feel able to use puppets, we are very easy to work with.*

Don't *let your audience see us asleep (ie. out of use) as it detracts from the overall impression.*

Do *use us with all ages and adapt what we say and how we act accordingly.*

Don't *use us for things that are too personal—it can make us feel a bit awkward.*

Do *use humour and add a bit of life.*

Don't *over-spiritualize what we say. We prefer to help illustrate the overall theme.*

Do *adapt us for all occasions; we are great for stories, sketches, notices, interviews, quizzes, announcements etc.*

Practical

Do *learn your script.*

Don't *forget what you want to say.*

Do *speak clearly.*

Don't *forget to move the mouth in time with what you are saying.*

Do *use the right voice with the right puppet.*

Do *remember you can say some very important things using us. . . people listen when we speak and they remember what we say for a long time.*

Don't *forget what the puppets (your arms) are doing—keep alert.*

Don't *forget to look at your audience when you talk to them, or at the other puppet if appropriate.*

Don't *stay up too long. . . !*

Using music

Teaching songs

Teaching new songs can be done in a number of ways. It can become tedious singing a song line by line, so try to avoid that whenever you can. However, it may be necessary to talk it through line by line when there are a lot of complicated actions. Even so, it is still worth singing it through if you have confident enough singers. This helps to draw the children in as they learn the song and gives them more confidence really to sing out.

Words need to be clearly visible. However, with action songs you need to avoid having to use song sheets or books. It is best to stick with the trusty overhead projector (OHP) whenever you can. If you are in a marquee, bereft of a power supply, then the words written out, clearly and in lower case, on card will do the job. Once the children have learnt the song, you can dispense with the cards. Their attention will then be focused on the person leading and, because they will be relying on their memory, they will remember the song for longer. This is especially worthwhile when you are teaching songs with a biblical message.

Different styles

Using variety in your music is important. However, if you want the children to remember the words of the songs, you will need to repeat them quite often. A variety of styles will add dimension, particularly when it comes to drawing the children into worship. It is not just adults who have the ability to worship; children too can enjoy a real sense of God's presence. Songs that are a little slower and more thoughtful and which describe God's greatness help to focus the children on our wonderful creator, saviour and friend. Make sure you maintain a careful balance in the style of the songs and they will become a special way for the children to learn about our wonderful God.

Finally, you might want to consider performing a song or two to the children. Performance songs appeal particularly to the older age ranges who can sometimes feel a bit embarrassed at joining in at first. If you have people with the ability, you could include a performance song in your presentation. Performance songs can often put the message across in a powerful way. Combine that with a mime that illustrates the words of the songs and you have a powerful tool which will draw the attention of most audiences.

Using your imagination

This section contains many useful ideas for you to use creatively in your programme.

Tops and tails

The very beginning and the very end of each session might seem not to warrant particular attention, but it is worth putting thought into it. It is very important to make the children feel welcome when they arrive, particularly the younger ones, as it can affect the way they feel for the next 30–40 minutes as they settle into new surroundings. If possible, have two or three people on the entrances to be 'smiley greeters' when people arrive—don't forget to be polite to parents too! Use a welcoming phrase or action at the beginning of each session to get everyone's attention and draw them into what is happening at the front. You could try using an enthusiastic greeting, such as: 'Gooood morning, everyone!'

When the children leave, it is often good to have them focused at the front for the last few minutes. Use this time to reiterate the main things taught during the day. Before they leave remind them about any specifics for the next day—what time to arrive, what to bring etc; and then make sure they have all their belongings before they leave. Leaders should be available to welcome the parents and guardians as they arrive to collect their charges, and bid farewell to the children as they leave.

Warm-ups

A decidedly untheological start to the day! It does work wonders, though, when it comes to directing the children's attention to what is going on at the front. Not only that, but it provides an easy and unembarrassing means by which late-comers can slip in and join in with what is going on. The basic idea is to use fairly loud, bouncy music as a background for plenty of silly, energy-sapping actions. This helps settle the children down for any stage-based programme that is to follow. Beware, though—you will often find the children outlasting the leaders!

Theme illustrations

Theme illustrations are well worth the time they take to prepare. They should be kept fairly short and most definitely simple. The basic idea is to provide a visual introduction to the day's teaching, pitched at an average age group. They do, of course, work just as well later in the programme, where they can reinforce what has gone before. Try wherever possible to use things that will involve your audience. That could mean watching a simple drama, or being part of it; going into the audience, asking questions or getting someone up front to be involved. Remember keep it short, simple and not too tenuous!

Adventure stories

Adventure stories are an excellent way to illustrate the theme. They reflect the theme for the day by drawing the children into a serialized adventure with a gripping cliff-hanger ending each day. In practice they are a lot of fun to perform, with the freedom really to ham it up, and provide a slightly lighter element to the programme (especially where the Watt family are involved—see Big Top and Starship Discovery themes). They not only lend themselves well to being dramatized, but also to being told imaginatively. How you use them will depend largely on who you have available and the gifts they have. Be ready for the moans of disappointment when you inform your audience that they will have to wait until tomorrow to find out what happens next!

Quizzes

Quizzes are by no means just a time-filler in the programme. However, be warned, because they nearly always take longer than you expect! Quizzes are a really useful way to recap the important aspects of the programme that have happened in the previous session or day(s). However, if you concentrate solely on biblical questions there is a danger the children will switch off, so do use a variety of questions. Engage in the children's culture a little bit. Find out what they are interested in and devise some questions which draw on their interests and key in to current topics of conversation. One word of warning: whatever you do, be seen to be fair! With dozens of competitive eyes and ears watching and listening you will be picked up on anything that is not fair!

Ideas for quizzes

Divide your audience in to two teams. Use simple, straightforward questions. Make sure you give each side equal opportunity to answer.

- *Bible Picture Pairs. Create two sets of cards, one set with Bible characters, the other with picture clues. e.g. Daniel and a lion. Number the back of one set and put letters on the other. The teams have to pick a number and letter to try and match the pairs. Points are given for correct pairs.*

- *Bible Story Quiz. Read a short Bible story from the Good News Bible, taking great care over the words. Re-read it, this time making obvious mistakes on specific words. Have the correct words written on an OHP and invite the teams to fit the correct word into its rightful place.*

- *Guess the Drawing. Set up a black or white board for each team, each with a quick draw artist and a hand spotter. Each artist has a list of Bible stories to draw (e.g. Noah and the Ark), but in differing orders. The first team to correctly guess all of them wins. Don't worry too much over artistic ability—often the less able they are, the funnier it gets!*

Ideas for scoring

- *Straightforward tally system with a marker for each team—try to relate it to the theme you are using (e.g. boats crossing an ocean, for the Adventure Cruise).*

- *Dress up a leader with a different item of clothing for each answer. Either the first fully garmented leader, or the one wearing the most at the end wins. (The leaders could start off attired in comical undergarments, such as brightly coloured long-johns and stripy vests.)*

- *Have a variety of different lengths of string or wool handy, with only one end visible. Each correct answer entitles the child to pick a piece for their team. Each team ties all the pieces they win together and the team with the longest overall length wins.*

● *If you have no scoreboard, or lack time, why not simply invite each child who has answered correctly onto the stage to act as a 'human tally' system. The team with the most members on stage are the winners.*

Using an overhead projector

A humble tool an overhead projector may be, but all too often it is used solely for showing only the most basic of words or pictures. Add a little imagination and you'd be amazed how useful it can be. Add a photocopier (and heat resistant acetates) and you don't need to worry about the quality of your artwork or copying abilities!

You do need to take care of your lettering. Use upper and lower case, not all capitals and not joined up. Don't make the lettering too small or thin and use clear visible colours (i.e blue or black— not yellow). On the subject of visibility, be careful where you place your screens if you are using a marquee—glare can really thin out the clarity of your image.

You might like to consider projecting images from your overhead projector on to a backdrop, which can then be used as an outline to create a larger-than-life painting screen. This method will prevent you having to struggle to paint a well-proportioned backdrop or large picture yourself. Just draw a scaled down version on an acetate. Then project it up where you want it and adjust the size by moving the overhead projector. Happy painting!

Finally, have you ever wanted large backdrops for dramas or stories which require quick scene changes? Simple! Hang a sheet, place the overhead projector behind it and project it forward. It will give you an instant backdrop to perform in front of. Scenes can change as quickly as you can move the acetates! So dig that old lump out from your church hall and get using it—creatively!

Discipline

Always a tricky one at a holiday club. After all, the emphasis is on having fun, isn't it? The trouble is that, without a level of discipline, a few can ruin the fun for the rest. Most teachers will tell you that it is easy to 'hype' the children up, but not so easy to bring them down again. It is, therefore, very important to maintain a level of control from the front, without the children necessarily noticing that you want them to be quiet and listen.

For many years, John and I have used some very simple 'action' words that focus the children's attention on what we are doing and quietening them in the process. Here are a few suggestions (encourage them to respond to your commands as quickly as they can).

● *STRAIGHT: Sit (or stand) up straight, arms folded and mouth closed.*

● *SERIOUS: Hands on one knee and no smiling! (Very serious!)*

● *SILLY: Any silly face will do!*

● *SLEEPY: A quick yawn and a stretch, and usually straight back to 'straight' again.*

Just to add a bit of variety, you could try throwing in a few waves too, such as:

● *BRAINWAVE: Waving hand on top of head.*

● *MICROWAVE: Little fingers only*

● *SHORTWAVE: Hand waving close to chest.*

● *MEDIUMWAVE: As above, but arm half out-stretched.*

● *LONGWAVE: As above, arm fully outstretched.*

I could go on, but I think you get the idea! You'll probably be able to think up a few of your own! Snap quickly between a few 'actions', usually ending with 'straight' and, as if by magic, everyone will be expectantly waiting to see what happens next.

Finally, here are some suggestions for maintaining control during the stage-based presentation:

● *Keep a sense of vitality to all you do—children are easily distracted.*

● *Supply plenty of opportunities for interaction. Involve the children in some of the stage-based fun.*

● *Keep things simple. Be bold, be big, be blatant!*

● *Use open questions to generate an interactive discussion. Use closed questions if you just want a simple 'yes' or 'no' answer.*

● *Provide plenty of fast-moving variety.*

● *Try to keep toilet visits to the rotation times (except in an emergency, of course!).*

Rotation

A quick word about how we suggest you plan things between the main stage-based teaching time. The general idea is to have a variety of 'static' activities that each group rotates between. As a guide, it is worth remembering to have the same number of activities as there are groups, but certainly not less. So with 2 groups, 2 activities; 3 groups, 3 activities etc. Bear in mind that the more groups you have, the more time the changeover will take and you'll therefore have less time for each individual activity.

Whenever possible split the children by age, rotate them, for example, between a game, a craft and a funsheet with a drink. If you have allocated one hour for the rotation time, this will give you about eighteen minutes per activity, with a couple of minutes 'manoeuvring' time as the groups move round (based on three groups). As the week goes on you may want to replace one of the funsheet sessions with an informal chat time, where the children can respond to the things they have been learning about.

Games

Games are an important element of any holiday club. They are designed to add an element of fun. You can tie them in to whichever theme you are using and link them to the overall 'flavour' of the week. For example, if your particular day's theme is 'trust' then develop a simple trust game where groups have to work together and help each other out. Games provide an important safety valve to dissipate all that energy that is stored up when children are in a confined space for more than ten minutes—it's quite a pressure tank!

Think about the practical aspects when planning your games. Do you envisage being indoors or out of doors? What will you do if it is wet? How much space do you have? How many children do you expect? How do you intend to gear the games to the different ages? How many leaders will there be to help? All these questions need considering *before* you start! Look at the games ideas in Part 2.

Crafts

As with games, crafts need to be tailored to the children's ages and abilities. You'll need far more preparation time with the younger members of your group if you haven't tailored the crafts to their needs. Craft time is not just another activity to keep the children happy, but a useful tool to help children relate to Christianity and the week's teaching. There are craft ideas with each theme in Part 2.

Funsheets

The emphasis is on the word *fun*! Don't make your funsheets too school-like. Take a look at the puzzle books and magazines that children read and base them on those. Funsheets should be an entertaining way to revise the Bible stories and memory verses used in the day's teaching, not a chore! There are funsheets for you to copy in Part 2.

Prayer

Make sure your prayers use language suited to the age of your children—with no long sentences or difficult words. Keep prayers short and to the point. Find ways of involving the children, possibly by having a repetitive phrase that can be said after each line of the prayer. You might like to try the teaspoon method if you have enough time—TSP: Thank you, Sorry, Please—a good order for all our prayers! Ask the children for items to pray for under each heading—three for each is a good number. When you prepare the children for prayer it can be helpful to use a 'countdown', for example, 1. Fold your arms, 2. Bow your head, 3. Close your eyes. Not theological—but helpful!

When The Time Comes

. . .When children respond to Jesus.

During your holiday club you may well find that children want to respond to the gospel message. Holiday clubs are all about sowing seeds and on many occasions God is gracious enough to allow us to see some of the reaping. It is therefore important that we should be prepared. Children know instinctively whether they are truly valued by those looking after them. A story which illustrates this is the tale of a poor boy who lived at the turn of the century. He would walk for miles, barefoot, to go to Sunday school, passing many other churches on the way. When asked why he did this he answered 'because they love me here'. Leading children to Christ is not just a task for theologically trained experts. The main credentials are a love for children and a realization that their decision is as valid before God as anyone's. It is important to remember that no one becomes a Christian through amazing counselling techniques or by the strength of an argument. God may use these things, but ultimately the process of conversion is the work of the Holy Spirit.

Some useful things to remember:

1. Be at ease and allow the child plenty of time to express their feelings.

2. Treat the child as an individual and be friendly.

3. Don't talk down to the child.

4. Don't do all the talking. Listen to what the child has to say.

5. Don't put words into the child's mouth. Ask questions which help them to think through their response.

Practical Points:

1. *Never disciple a child behind closed doors. A quiet corner of the main room, perhaps with some scatter cushions for comfort, would make a suitably informal area.*

2. *In order to avoid unnecessary complications or misunderstandings, it is important to disciple children of the same sex as yourself.*

3. *Spend a little time beforehand summarizing your own conversion experience so that you communicate simply and confidently with the child.*

4. *Prepare your own way of explaining the gospel using simple illustrations and language or find a suitable leaflet which explains Christian basics at the right level.*

Many people become Christians in their childhood and are living testimonies of the fact that God can work in young lives. Children are probably at their most receptive between the ages of 5 and 12. They are also much more vulnerable and able to be easily led or overwhelmed at this age, so tread carefully! Anyone taking an upfront role is in a position of influence which makes it very easy to allow one's personality to get in the way, thus lessening the impact of the Holy Spirit. If this happens you may, on the surface, appear to have good results with children making a profession of 'faith'; but if the impact arises more from our own influence rather than Christ's, it will not last. Don't expect a child to grasp totally all that the Christian life involves, faith is an ongoing and ongrowing process.

A child's understanding of the gospel will depend a lot upon their background and upbringing. For example, if a child has been brought up in a home where the parents or guardians have no time for the child then s/he might struggle to understand that someone s/he *can't* see not only has time for them, but has a deep love too. Similarly, the perspective we have of our earthly father has a profound effect on how we see our heavenly father.

Most children, however, will be able to grasp a basic understanding of what Christianity means, namely:

1. *The things we do wrong separate us from God.*

2. *When Jesus died he made it possible for us to be friends with God.*

3. *When Jesus rose again from the dead he made it possible for us to be with God for ever.*

4. *God knows, and wants, the best for us, his children. The Bible tells us how he wants us to live.*

5. *God has promised never to leave us and we can look forward to being with him for ever.*

It is important to reinforce your teaching with biblical examples.

No two children will respond to the gospel message in the same way. It is important to allow the child to explain in their own words what they have learnt, this will give you a fair analysis of their level of understanding. Encourage them to talk to God simply and in their own way. Their prayer might be unconventional, but resist the temptation to jump in and correct them. If the prayer is real and from the heart, that is the response that God wants to hear, no matter how unconventional. Some children may ask you to pray for them, and then echo that prayer themselves. However they respond, an individual and personal experience should be encouraged.

Children will often respond by saying sorry to Jesus and asking him to be their friend. It is important, however, to encourage the child to see Jesus as a very special friend who is also our Saviour. We come to the Lord Jesus Christ, bow before him and acknowledge him as Lord, Saviour and King, who comes into our lives to live right inside us by his Spirit.

Follow-up

Here are some practical guidelines to help you establish your own follow-up programme:

1. *Encourage the child to tell someone about their new-found faith—perhaps a holiday club leader, Sunday school teacher or a Christian parent.*

2. *Encourage the child to read the Bible. Find out if they have a Bible of their own. The Good News Bible is the easiest to understand. Give them some guidance as to how to set about reading their Bible and have some suitable study notes ready to offer them.*

3. *Where necessary link the child to a suitable group in their local church. For children unable to attend regularly, the Dynamite Club offers an alternative as a postal Sunday school. Membership is free and each child receives a monthly pack of studies including quizzes, puzzles, etc., which they can send back when completed. The material can be used equally as an addition to an existing Sunday school programme. Details of how you can contact the Dynamite Club are given in the 'Which Resources?' appendix on page 145.*

4. *Contact the child's parents or guardians and invite them to any church-based events aimed at the family.*

5. *Keep in contact with the child, perhaps sending them a set of study notes with a letter of encouragement.*

6. *If the child is a member of your church, try to build a good friendship with them and encourage them as they grow in their faith. Be available for them and remember that the quality of your own life will be a strong influence—BE A GOOD EXAMPLE!*

Finally, don't be disappointed if you find not many children respond to the gospel during or immediately after the holiday club. This doesn't mean nothing has been achieved—it may just be that your job was to sow seeds and lay the foundation—harvesting may come at another time. We should expect great things from our great God but also remember that his ways are not always ours.

Nurture groups

It is very important that children who have made a commitment to Christ following a holiday club or mission activity are encouraged to grow in their faith. They need to be provided with the opportunity to learn more about their new faith. This is particularly important if they are from an unchurched or non-Christian background. A nurture group can provide a suitable environment to help them.

In such a group you can:

1. *Reinforce the truths the children have learnt.*

2. *Provide a smooth transition from the holiday club in to the life of the church.*

3. *Provide an environment for the children to enjoy friendship and warmth with their peers.*

3. *Encourage the individual to begin to share and open up within the group.*

It is advisable to prepare for the formation of a nurture group well in advance of the holiday club. Choose a venue and decide on some suitable material to use over the coming weeks. Ideally, children should be invited to join a group near their home. Contact the parents and explain what the group is all about.

Preparation

1. *Leaders—preferably these should be people the children will know, such as their leaders from holiday club. The number of leaders will vary according to the number and ages of the children.*

2. *Group identity—choose a good name for the group, perhaps following on from the holiday club theme. It needs to sound (and be) fun.*

3. *Venue—there are various options here, e.g: the church or church hall, school (either lunchtime or the end of the day) or in a home.*

4. *Duration—This is up to you, but 45 minutes to an hour is the optimum time. Arrange a set number of meetings, advising children and parents/guardians accordingly. The series could end with a special Sunday Family Service where children are given their own Bibles.*

5. *Material—this needs to be chosen carefully. There is plenty of material on the market to choose from. The programme needs to be fun and could include an ice-breaker game, song, group activity and question time. You might feel it appropriate to end with a time of prayer.*

6. *Group size—six to eight people would be a good group size if everyone attends regularly, otherwise it might be better to have a maximum of twelve.*

Why not consider maintaining a regular ongoing children's club that carries on from where your nurture group leaves off? This provides you with an ideal way in to the whole life of the church.

PART TWO

How To Do It!

This section contains three ready-to-use holiday club thematic outlines. Each day's teaching contains a number of different elements for you to pick and mix into your own programme. Below is a suggested timetable which will fit any of the themes. It gives you an idea of how to programme your day; it can be as flexible as you need.

The programme

These timetables can be used for either a 2 or a 2½ hour children's club. Alternatively, you can adapt the layout to suit your situation.

30 minutes before the start: the team meets for prayer (15 minutes).

15 minutes before the start: the club opens for registration.

2-hour programme

Section 1
(Stage-based—30 minutes)

0.00 Welcome and warm up

0.02 Theme song

0.07 Introduction to the theme (including theme illustration).

0.12 Action song

0.17 Drama/Adventure story (in daily installments)

0.25 Memory verse

0.30 Split for activities

Section 2
(1 hour of rotated activities)

2 or 3 activities with either:

2 x 30 minutes of games and crafts: 2 rotation groups

   or:

3 x 18 minutes of games, crafts, snack and chat, and fun sheets: 3 rotation groups

Section 3
(Stage-based—30 minutes)

1.30 Action song

1.35 Clowns

1.40 Performance song or puppet sketch

1.45 Bible story

1.53 Quiz and memory verse recap

1.58 Prayer

2.00 Theme song

2 ½ hour programme

Section 1 (Stage-based—1 hour)

0.00 Welcome and introduction

0.02 Warm up

0.04 Theme song

0.08 Theme illustration

0.13 Action songs

0.18 Drama/Adventure story

0.26 Memory verse

0.32 Quiz

0.42 Puppets

0.48 Bible story

1.00 Split for activities

Section 2 (1 hour of rotated activities)

2 or 3 activities with either:

2 x 30 minutes of games and crafts: 2 rotation
groups

or:

3 x 18 minutes of games, crafts, snack and chat,
and funsheets: 3 rotation groups

Section 3 (Stage-based—30 minutes)

2.00 Welcome back

2.02 Clowns/action songs

2.17 Quiz 2 and memory verse recap

2.25 Song

2.28 Prayer

2.30 Theme song

The elements

Welcome You will find helpful suggestions
on how to welcome children in Part One
'Using your imagination' on page 19.

Warm up A quick energy-releasing kick-
off, which draws their attention to the
stage and prepares them for what is to
come.

Theme Song The sheet music for these can
be found in Appendix B on page 146. All
the songs for the three themes are can be
found on the Ultimate Holiday Club Guide
cassette, which is available from your local
Christian bookshop or, in cases of difficulty,
direct from BRF.

Illustration The illustration helps to earth
the theme in a fun and practical way.

Teaching/action songs Ready-to-use
sheet music can be found in Appendix B on
page 146.

Drama/Adventure story A daily cliff-
hanging adventure in theme-related
installments. The story can either be read
as a story, performed as a drama or
adapted to your own style.

Memory verse This shows where in the
Bible we learn the truth of the day's
theme. A paraphrase of the verse may
sometimes be used in order to give it the
correct rhythm.

Quiz Suggestions and ideas for using
quizzes can be found in Part One 'Using
your imagination' on page 19. Don't forget
to include a few questions that relate to
the programme so far.

Puppets The continuing adventures of Bert
and Lucy relate the day's theme in a
memorable way using a short, light-
hearted skit.

Bible Story Containing the main thrust of
the day's teaching. The style selections can
either be learnt by heart and performed as
a sketch, or adapted to your own style.

Rotation time Including games, crafts,
video, drama, snack and chat and
funsheets.

Welcome back

Clowns A light-hearted perception of life
and the universe!

Song(s) See Part One, page 19.

Quiz 2/Memory verse recap A valuable
opportunity to re-enforce the main points of
the day's teaching.

Prayer A brief opportunity for the children
to close their physical eyes and open their
spiritual ones.

Theme song Repeated here to round off
the day.

Theme 1: The Adventure Cruise

Setting up

Choose crew member names and appropriate dress for your leaders and assistants. You'll need craft leaders and sports crew to lead crafts and games, a deck manager to oversee sessions and floaters to assist with general running of sessions. Choose team colours and names to match the theme. Decorate your venue in keeping with the theme. The room could be a ship, with flags and bunting, a ship's wheel, bell, lifebuoys, portholes, main deck, bridge, galley etc. A frieze can be compiled over the course of the sessions to decorate the walls. Don't forget to design handouts for the final session if you are holding a 'Sunday Deck Celebration' so that children can invite their relatives and friends.

Overview

The Adventure Cruise opens a window to characters from the Bible, looking at the CHOICES they had to make, how they could CALL on Jesus, (and also how Jesus called ordinary people to himself), how their lives were CHANGED as result and the COMMITMENT and COST involved in following Jesus.

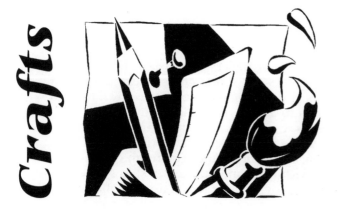

Crafts

Sailor's hats

For each child you will need:

White card 55 cm x 15 cm

Circle of card 25 cm diameter

2 strips of ribbon 15 cm each

Shirring elastic

1. Write ship's name on white card and decorate.
2. Make regular cuts along one edge, 3 cm deep.
3. Glue the edges of strip of card together to form a ring.
4. Bend cut edge inwards.
5. Glue circle of card onto bent edge of ring.
6. Glue ribbons to the top of the back of hat.
7. Make small holes in base of hat (place clear sticky tape where you intend to make the hole to prevent the card from tearing and use a hole-punch to make the hole). Thread shirring elastic through holes to finish hat.

1

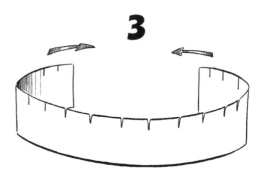

H.M.S. ADVENTURE

2

3

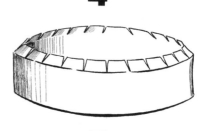

4

5

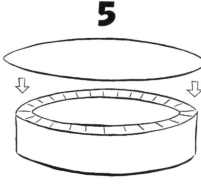

6

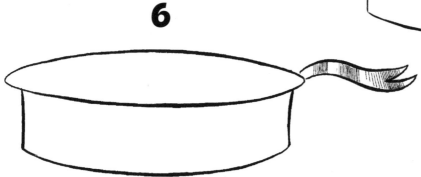

Sailing boats

For each child you will need:

Template photocopied or traced onto card

Glue

1. Cut out boat.
2. Colour in/decorate.
3. Glue corresponding tabs to each other.

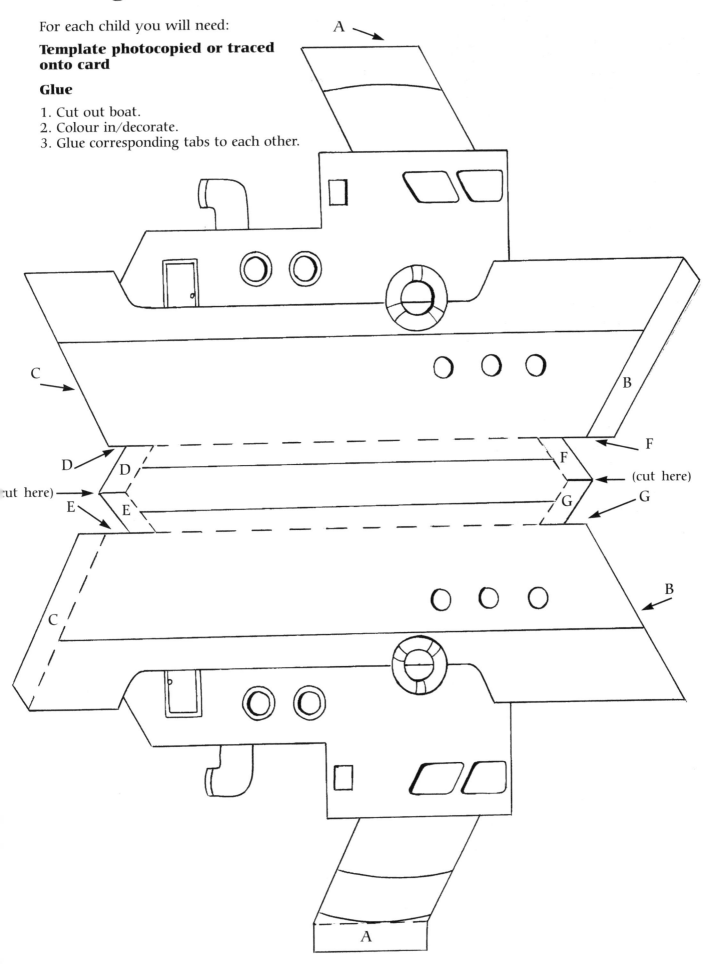

Fishing games

For each child you will need:

White card 60 cm x 25 cm

Circle of card 25 cm diameter

card for fish

2 paper clips

drinking straw

50 cm thin string

1. Decorate one side of the card with underwater scene.
2. Glue edges together to form tube, with decoration on the outside.
3. Cut slashes in card circle, 3 cm deep.
4. Fold slashes inwards and glue to base.
5. Cut out fish, using template.
6. Colour fish. Slide paper clip onto fish's nose and bend clip up.
7. Thread string through straw and secure at one end with sticky tape.
8. Fasten paper clip to other end of string. Form into hook.

Memory verse choosers

For each child you will need:

Piece of cartridge paper, 21 cm square

1. Fold paper in half and in half again. Open out.
2. Fold points to middle.
3. Turn over and fold new points to middle.
4. Turn over and pull out flaps.
5. Open out and on inside flaps write:

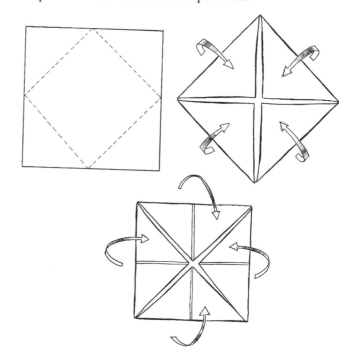

Fish template

I will always be with you.

I will never turn anyone away who comes to me.

Everyone who calls on the name of the Lord shall be saved.

The old has gone and the new has come.

All who love God must also love their brother and sister.

Forget self and follow me!

We change!

Consider the cost!

6. Fold in and on corresponding flaps write

trust   choose   Saviour   changed

committed   cost   Zacchaeus

The rich young man

7. On outside flap. write:

red   yellow   green
blue

To use, choose a colour, then alternate the ways of opening the chooser as many times as there are letters in the word (i.e. three times for 'red'). Then do the same for the items on the inside flaps, but by number of syllables (i.e. three times for Zacchaeus). Then choose one of the flaps and read the verse beneath it.

Bunting

For each child you will need:

Scraps of fabric or card or paper

Template

String

1. Cut fabric using template as pattern.
2. Fold as illustrated.
3. Thread onto string to required length.

Treasure islands (made over two days)

For each child you will need:

Card egg box base

Newspaper

Flour and water paste

Paints

Plain paper

Scraps of coloured paper, shiny paper etc.

Glue

1. Mix flour and water to glue like consistency.
2. Tear newspaper into small pieces.
3. Cover egg box base with layers of paper mâché and allow to dry overnight.
4. Paint island scene onto dry paper mâché.
5. Make palm trees from strips of green paper, by rolling half an A4 sheet (cut lengthways) tightly and cutting slits in one end of the tube to about half way down to form the fronds. Then pull these out and curl with scissors. Affix to island by making a tab on the base.
6. Decorate with small paper shell shapes, blue shiny paper for river etc.

Flags

For each child you will need:

Book with pictures of flags or ideas for designs

Wooden candy floss stick or dowelling stick

Paper triangle or A4 sheet of paper

Glue

1. Decorate paper triangle with flag design.
2. Glue decorated flag to stick.

Adventure cruise jigsaws

For each child you will need:

Template on page opposite photocopied or traced onto paper

Colouring pencils

Glue

A4 sheet to make envelope

1. Colour picture.
2. Glue onto card.
3. Cut out following grey lines on illustration.
4. Fold A4 sheet in three to make C5 envelope. Staple or glue edges of pocket, leaving flap free. Decorate envelope and use to store jigsaw pieces.

Badges

For each child you will need:

Card circle 12 cm diameter

Safety pin (for older children) or sticky tape (for younger children)

Plain sticky label

1. Decorate card with appropriate design.
2. Write child's name on sticky label.
3. Use sticky tape to fix safety pin to back of card for older children. Just use a ring of sticky tape for younger children.

Frieze

You will need:

Rolls of unpasted wallpaper, or large sheets of card

Collage scraps (fabrics, shiny paper, corrugated card, plastic containers etc.)

Felt tipped pens or paints

Glue

1. Use paint and collage to illustrate each day's theme.
2. Build frieze day by day throughout the holiday club.
3. Display on walls so children can see frieze being 'built' as club progresses.

Games

Port and starboard

This game takes place on the deck of a ship—marked out by a rectangular boundary which is big enough for the children to run around in. Decide which side of your rectangle is going to be PORT and which STARBOARD.

Demonstrate the following commands to the children:

Climb the rigging: Pretend to climb.

Captain's coming: Stand to attention and salute.

Man overboard: Pretend to look (hand above eyes).

Scrub the decks: On hands and knees, scrubbing the floor.

Freeze: Freeze whichever position you happen to be in.

Bombs overhead: Curl up in a ball on the floor.

Submarines: Lie on back with one leg in the air.

Galley: Line up down the centre of the deck.

Hammock: Go to sleep.

When the children are familiar with the commands, and know which side of the ship is port and which is starboard, call out the commands in any order. When 'port' or 'starboard' are called the children have to run to the correct side of the room. The last two children to carry out the command or reach port or starboard are out of the game. Designate an area of the room as the crows' nest where the children who are out can sit and look out for the last two to carry out the commands among those still in the game.

Sea object-drawing game

Split the children into teams, with about eight in each team. Sit them down in their teams in a circle facing inwards. Give each team a piece of paper and a pencil.

Explain to them that they must all be able to see the piece of paper, so they need to sit close together. You have a list of objects all to do with the sea which the teams have to guess. Each team sends you a person to whom you whisper an item on the list. They then have to go back to their team and draw the item without giving any verbal clues. Once their team has guessed the object the next team member comes to you and, when they have told you what the object was, you whisper the next object to them, which they then have to draw for their team. It's a good idea to split your list into two or three units so that the teams are not all trying to guess the same object at the same time—otherwise verbal cheating can be a problem! Make sure the teams send their members up to you fairly so that everyone has a go—not just the best artists!

Objects to draw could include:

Rowing boat	Lilo
Beach ball	Yacht
Seagull	Wave
Shark	Seaweed
Sunset	Whale
Eel	Fishing rod
Lighthouse	Dog fish shell
Flippers	Ship's wheel
Cockle shell	Swimming hat
Fisherman's net	Starfish
Beach towel	Lifebuoy
Seahorse	Sandcastle
Sailor's hat	Submarine
Sandwich	Octopus
Crab	Coral reef
Anchor	Ship's biscuits
Jolly Roger	Bucket and spade
Luxury liner	Water wings
Telescope	Crow's nest
Salute	

All the fish in the sea

Make a large circle of chairs, with the chairs facing outwards. Children sit on the chairs. Each child is given the name of a fish in rotation, e.g. first child: cod; second: haddock; third: plaice. When you call the name of a fish all the children with that name get up and move round the circle in a clockwise direction according to the following commands:

The. . . went out for a swim: Those called get up and move round the circle in a clockwise direction.

All the fish in the sea went out for a swim: Everyone gets up.

Sea is calm: Walk

Sea is choppy: Skip

Sea is rough: Jump

Sea is stormy: Run fast

Tide turns: Change direction

Fishermen are coming: Children run in the direction they are going back to their own seat. The last child back to their seat is out and comes to sit in an area of the room you have designated as the fisherman's net.

When there is only one of each type of fish left, call out all the fish in the sea until you have an overall winner.

Sharks

Mark off a boundary in the room large enough for the children to run across. Ask all the children to go to one side of the room.

Tell them that they are little fish and they have to swim (run) across the sea to the other side. The only thing is that there is a mean old shark out there who likes to catch little fish.

Choose someone to be the shark. When you shout 'swim!' all the fish must try to get to the other side, but if the shark touches them they will be turned into pieces of seaweed. When they are caught by the shark they have to stand on the spot with their feet together and wave their stretched out arms from side to side.

Those who make it to the other side of the room wait for you to give the command 'Swim!', when they have to swim back across the room, but this time avoiding the seaweed as well as the shark. If they are caught by either the shark or a piece of seaweed, they, too become seaweed. Remember the children who are pieces of seaweed cannot move their feet.

This is repeated until everyone is caught. The winner is the one who manages to avoid the shark and the seaweed the longest. They then become the shark for the next game.

Net the fish

Cut at least eight bath sponges into fish shapes.

Split the children into equal teams of no more than ten per team. Sit the teams in different corners of the room.

Give each team member a number from 1–10, giving the youngest members the lower numbers and the older members the higher numbers. Give each team a tray and place the sponge fish in the centre of the room.

When you call out a number, everyone with that number has to collect four fish for their team. They are only allowed to collect one fish at a time. They must first collect their fish from the middle of the room, taking them back one at a time to their team's tray and then, when the fish in the middle are gone, they can take a fish from someone else's tray and take it back to their own. The winning team is the one which manages to collect all four fish first.

It's important to have a leader in each team to spot when the team gets the four fish, because the fourth fish may be taken away in a split second and no one will notice that they were the winners! The runners are not allowed to snatch the fish out of other team runners hands and the rest of the team are not allowed to help in any way, neither are they allowed to stop someone taking a fish off their team's tray.

When you have a winner, call out another number and so on, until everyone has had a turn.

Who's captain?

Stand the children in a circle, facing inwards. Choose one child to go out of the room, and another to be the ship's captain. Call the first child back in. The captain leads the others by miming an action, for example:

Saluting, swimming strokes (crawl, doggy paddle, breaststroke, backstroke etc.), fishing, scrubbing the decks, climbing the rigging etc. The first child has to try to work out who the captain is as the actions change.

Un-knot the nets!

Split the children into teams of not more than twelve per team, forming a circle facing inwards. Ask the teams to hold the hand of someone else in their team, but not the person next to them. All the children should eventually be joined together in their teams with no free hands. Now ask them to un-knot the net—to unravel themselves without letting go of any hands— until they are once more formed into a circle facing inwards. This game can be played as a race.

Hook a fish!

Split the children into four or more teams of no more than 10 per team. Make enough fishing lines with a hook for each team.

Cut the tops off at least twelve one-litre squash bottles and paper-clip them all together. Make the same number of cardboard fish and stand them in the bottles. (See diagram). Give

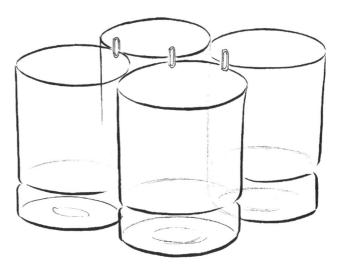

each team a bucket, a fishing rod and a chair. Place the rod and bucket on the chair, away from the team and put the squash bottles and fish in the middle of the room. Number the team members from 1–10.

When you call out a number, all the team members with that number dash to their chair, pick up their rod and go to the middle to try and hook a fish. Once they have hooked one, they have to take it (still on the rod) and put it in their bucket. Set a time limit of, say, 45 seconds. After that time, count up the number of fish hooked for each team. Each team keeps account of the number of fish hooked by each of their members. Call out another number until all the players have had a turn. Tot up the final score for each team.

Day 1

 CHOICE—Jesus chooses to respond to a cry for help.

 John 6:37 'I will never turn away anyone who comes to me.'

 When we choose to turn to Jesus he will not let us down. A man with leprosy does just that and Jesus chooses to reach out, touch and heal him. Jesus won't hesitate to help when we turn to him and he longs to make us whole.

Day 2

 CALL—Blind Bartimaeus calls out for help.

 Romans 10:13 'Everyone who calls on the name of the Lord shall be saved.'

 Blind Bartimaeus was considered unimportant by those around him. When he called out to Jesus for help, Jesus didn't ignore him, but responded to his call. Each of us is equally important to God and God hears us when we call out to him for help.

Day 3

 CHANGE—Zacchaeus' life-changing encounter with Jesus.

 2 Corinthians 5:17 'When anyone is joined to Christ he is a new creation, the old has gone and the new has come.'

 Zacchaeus was a rich but lonely man. When Jesus chose to spend time with him it gave his life a new purpose. We can find this purpose too when we let Jesus into our lives. We change!

Day 4

 COMMITMENT—The paralysed man and his four committed friends.

 1 John 4:21 'All who love God must also love their brother and their sister.'

 The four friends were committed to bringing their paralysed friend to meet Jesus. It wasn't easy, but they persevered. The Christian life is a journey full of excitement and difficulties. God wants us to help each other along the way.

Day 5

 COST—The rich young man finds the cost of following Jesus too great.

 Matthew 16:24 'If anyone wants to come with me, he must forget self, carry his cross, and follow me.'

 The rich young man considered the cost but missed out on a great opportunity. If we truly want to follow Jesus we must consider the cost carefully and be prepared to give up whatever he asks us to.

Day 1
CHOICE

Jesus chooses to respond to a cry for help

Aim

To show that when we choose to come to Jesus he will not turn us away.

Warm up

'Abandon Ship' by Richard Hubbard. A fast-moving song, ideal for warming up. The song is on the ICC tape *Spring Harvest Kids' Praise*, Cat. No. SH9589, price £4.99. ICC's address can be found in the 'Which Resources?' appendix on page 145.

Theme song

The theme song is *The Adventure Cruise*. The sheet music can be found in Appendix B on page 146. The song can be found on the *Ultimate Holiday Club Guide* cassette, available from your local Christian bookshop, or, in case of difficulty, direct from BRF.

Theme illustration: Grandma's Gunky Gunge

Make up a jar of Grandma's Gunky Gunge, either using purchased 'gunge' from a toy shop, or making your own by heating a weak cornflour and water paste until it thickens, adding food colouring to get the lurid colour and washing up liquid to give it that slippery feel. You can also use a watered-down jelly mixture. Put a small coin into the jar and hide the jar from your audience. Invite a volunteer on to the stage and ask them if they would like the coin. When they say 'yes', tell them that it's theirs for the keeping—but they have to get it out of the jar. Now they have the choice. Is it worth their while to go for the coin or not? Point out that we are much more valuable than a coin, and Jesus chose to come into a messed-up world to rescue us.

Drama/ Adventure story

The adventures of Sid and Basher: 1

This is a four-part contemporary story which picks up the teaching for the week, revealing it in daily installments. The story outline can be adapted to be performed as a drama, dramatized narration, or read as a story. Feel free to embellish and adapt the outline to suit your own situation.

Sid's gran has won a competition. The prize is a week's cruise on a luxury liner. As the summer holidays are coming up she asks Sid if he'd like to come along. Sid can bring a friend with him. Who will he choose? He decides to choose his good friend, Basher, a fun guy who's a bit of a crazy dude.

The cruise is full of very rich and snooty people. Poor Sid and Basher have quite a struggle fitting in. One night, during the evening meal (a very posh affair) the lights suddenly go out and when they come back on again everyone starts screaming,

'I've been robbed!!' Even Sid's gran has had her necklace stolen.

Sid and Basher decide it's time to have a good look round this luxury liner, so they start to explore the ship. They split up, arranging to report back by the swimming pool in half an hour's time. Sid is exploring a corridor when he notices that one of the cabin doors is slightly ajar. He sees a dim light coming from the cabin and hears muffled voices. He tiptoes up to the door just in time to overhear the words, 'Where're we goin' to stash the stuff, then?' followed by a gruff, 'We need to sort it out later, we must have a least £200,000's worth!'

Sid leans closer to the door, straining his ear hear the phrase, 'So where're we gonna hide it?' But Sid leans too far. The door suddenly falls open and Sid falls into the room—landing ungracefully in a heap at a pair of enormous feet. Sid feels himself grabbed and jerked into the air.

'What 'ave we 'ere, then? A prying little 'Arry, eh?'

Sid is about to answer that his name is Sid, not 'Arry, but he finds himself part of their discussion.

''ow much do'y think 'e 'eard?'

'What are we gonna do with him?'

Then they seem to come to a decision. Setting him down on his feet, but not letting go of him, the man who seems to be the boss says,

'Look, kid, you've got a choice; you either keep your mouth shut and we'll let you go— but if you blab to your family you're in for it— or we tie you up and we may throw you overboard if people start looking for you. Do you hear what I'm saying!! Do you know what I mean???'

Sid does hear and he does know what is meant, so he makes his decision. He stamps as hard as he can on the man's foot and runs towards the door. But just as he thinks he's got away. . . YOU'LL HAVE TO WAIT UNTIL TOMORROW TO FIND OUT WHAT HAPPENS!

Drama/Adventure story link

Sid had to make a choice about the tricky situation he was in. Neither choice looked very good. We all have to make choices every day; sometimes big and sometimes small. Jesus gives us the choice of whether to follow him or not— that is an important choice and one that no one else can make for us.

Memory verse

John 6:37 'I will never turn away anyone who comes to me.'

A rap: I will never//turn away//anyone//who comes to me

/ = clap

A song: The sheet music can be found in Appendix B on page 146. The song can be found on the *Ultimate Holiday Club Guide* cassette, available from your local Christian bookshop, or, in case of difficulty, direct from BRF.

Quiz

Questions could include:

Which film does the song 'I wanna be like you' come from?
Jungle Book

Who is the odd one out. . . Take That, Cliff Richard, Blur, John Major?
John Major

Who won a week's cruise on a luxury liner?
Sid's gran

Who's the odd one out. . . Eric Cantona, Paul McGrath, Rowan Atkinson, Ryan Giggs?
Rowan Atkinson

Puppets

Lucy: (*calling out*) Bert! Bert! Oh, I'm glad I've found you!

Bert: Lucy! You made me jump! What is it?

Lucy: I've just found the tickets I thought I'd lost for the Wanderers' match.

Bert: Oh good! I expect you're glad you found them.

Lucy: Of course! It's going to be brilliant to see them. You will come with me, Bert, won't you?

Bert: Me? Wow! Yes, that would be great!

Lucy: I do love the Wanderers. I think I'm going to play for them when I grow up.

Bert: I don't think you'll ever grow up, Lucy! Anyway, you'd have to be really good to play for them.

Lucy: I know, but I am good and if I keep practising, I'm sure I'll be able to.

Bert: Who are they playing, anyway?

Lucy: Er. . . I think it's United.

Bert: United?

Lucy: Yes, that's right.

Bert: But they played Wanderers last Saturday!

Lucy: Last Saturday?

Bert: Yes—don't tell me you got the dates mixed up, Lucy!

Lucy: Er. . . well. . . um. . .

Bert: I don't believe it—you've missed the date!

Lucy: Oh dear.

Bert: You are silly sometimes, Lucy. Come on, let's go and play.

Lucy: OK. Bye, everyone.

Bert: Bye, bye.

Bible story

Jesus responds to a cry for help. Read the accounts in Matthew 8:1–4, Mark 1:40–45 and Luke 5:12–16 (Jesus heals a man).

Key points

● *The man knew that Jesus could heal him, but was unsure about Jesus' willingness to do so.*

● *Jesus doesn't hesitate to help when we choose to turn to him.*

● *Jesus longs to heal us and make us clean.*

Style suggestion

Cast: Narrator and two others (A and B)

Narr: There were lots of unpopular people in the Bible— the Romans, for example. . .

(*A steps forward and pretends to be a soldier*). They were the enemy, the invaders, who had taken away the Jews' freedom. So the Jews hated them. . . (*B pulls faces and sticks out tongue at A*).

A: Then there were the tax collectors. . . (*Narrator steps forward and mimes being a tax collector trying to get money from B*). They took people's money and gave it to the Romans! (*Narrator mimes taking money from B and giving it to A*). So the Jews hated them. . . (*B pulls faces and sticks out tongue at Narrator*).

Narr: But there were other people who were just as unpopular.

A: But they weren't the enemy, like the Romans!

B: But they didn't cheat like the tax collectors!

Narr: No, in fact they hadn't done anything against the people. But when the people saw them coming they would shout. . .

A: GET AWAY!

Narr: Some people even picked up stones and hurled them at these people. (*A and B mime throwing stones and start to shout 'Get away!'*)

B: But why?

Narr: Because they were ill.

B: Ill! Then they should have helped them and been kind—not thrown stones and shouted at them!

Narr: They had a dreaded skin disease— probably leprosy. The skin would have patchy white sections, it would be sore and would start to flake off.

A: The person would gradually become weaker and weaker and eventually they would die. There was no cure.

B: The people believed that if they touched anything that the leper had touched then they would catch the disease too.

Narr: One day a man with this dreaded skin disease started to come towards Jesus.

A looks panic-stricken. B mimes walking slowly towards Narrator. A runs behind Narrator, looking horrified.

A: GET AWAY! (*A mimes picking up a stone and throwing it at B*).

Narr: No! Neither Jesus nor his disciples shouted 'Get away!'—nor did they throw stones at him.

A: Oh! Right! I know what they did! 'RUN!'

Narr: No! The man knelt down close to Jesus (*B kneels at Narrator's feet*) and said. . .

B: If you want to, you can make me clean.

A: Well, he doesn't! So push off!

Narr: Jesus could have said that, but he didn't. He was filled with pity for this man. He *chose* to help him. He stretched out his hand and touched him. (*Narrator reaches out to touch B*).

A: HE DID WHAT?!?! Didn't he know he could catch the disease?!?!

Narr: Of course he did, but he also knew that this man hadn't been touched by another human being for a long, long time. So Jesus *chose* to touch him. He said, 'Be clean.'

B: At once the disease left the man, and he was clean. (*He rises, looking at the skin on his arms and legs and looking jolly excited*).

Narr: Jesus told him to go to the priest and let him examine him—but not to tell anyone. But of course the man did—he told everyone he met about the great thing Jesus had done for him. Jesus hadn't rejected him like other people had. Jesus had chosen to heal him.

A: Even if everyone else rejects you and turns away from you. . .

Narr: . . . Jesus never turns away *anyone* who comes to him.

Quiz 2, memory verse recap, prayer and theme song

The Adventure Cruise

CHOICE—*Jesus chooses to respond to a cry for help*

Choose the safest route for the ship to get to the harbour

 *Find the words of today's memory verse in the wordsearch and write them on the lines. The letters and numbers that are left will tell you where in the Bible the verse comes from.*

```
J  r  e  v  e  n
o  c  t  u  r  n
e  n  o  y  n  a
h  n  a  m  b  V
3  w  h  o  e  7
a  l  l  i  w  s
```

anyone away comes never to turn who will

I _ _ _ _   _ _ _ _ _   _ _ _ _   _ _ _ _   _ _ _ _ _   _ _ _   _ _ _ _ _   _ _ m e

_ _ _ _   _ v _ _

Which person does Jesus turn away?
(answer at bottom of sheet)

 **What choices do you have to make each day?**
What choices are easy?
What choices are hard?
How do our choices change things?

Using the two boxes, show what can happen when we either make a good choice or a bad choice.

Good choices	Bad choices

Day 2

CALL

Blind Bartimaeus calls out for help

Aim

To show that it doesn't matter who you are, but when you call on God, he always responds—and sometimes in an amazing way.

Warm up

See Day 1

Theme song

See Day 1

Theme illustration 1

You'll need a pair of toy handcuffs that require a key. This simple illustration uses mime to communicate the message that we often get ourselves stuck with a problem that we can't solve on our own. Often the only solution is to call out to someone else for help.

'A' is busy preparing something side on to the audience, B appears, doesn't want to disturb A, but his attention is drawn to a shiny object sticking out of A's back pocket. B sneaks up behind and slowly pulls out a pair of handcuffs. B is immediately entranced by this new-found toy and becomes engrossed in playing with it, resulting in his own hands being locked in the cuffs. A meanwhile discovers the handcuffs are missing and proceeds to look for them, oblivious to B's presence. B's vain attempt to free himself leads to his calling out for help. (This is done in mime by simply raising cupped hands to mouth.)

A immediately turns round and in annoyance spots the whereabouts of his handcuffs. However, he can't help but laugh at B's predicament. B, looking very sorry for himself, holds his hands out to A in hope of help. A smiles and duly produces the key from his pocket, wags his finger at B, but then releases him. At this point the leader can briefly recap the scenario, highlighting the fact that God always hears our call for help and responds in the way which is best for us.

Theme illustration 2

An alternative, but more well-known mime is the 'Do not touch' mime.

Character A (male) comes onto the stage and spots a chair facing away from the audience with a sign hanging on the back saying, 'DO NOT TOUCH'. A's natural inquisitiveness leads him to inspect the chair, whereupon he discovers the sign. After a moment's pause a wry grin spreads across his face. He nonchalantly flicks the sign onto the floor and begins to toy with the idea of touching the chair, getting closer and closer until eventually one hand touches the chair and becomes stuck to the back. At this point Character B (female) appears from stage right, spots Character A immediately, recognizes him and approaches, waving. They smile at each other and then B offers a hand of friendship to A. They do a hand slap. B continues on her way, exiting stage left. A panics and struggles to release his hand. In attempting to do so he places his other hand on the back of the chair, only to find that too becomes firmly stuck. After a few moments' struggle with both hands on the chair, which could include A raising the chair off the ground, he slumps down, straddling the chair in defeat. Now he's well and truly glued!

Character B re-enters from stage left, spots A and immediately heads towards him. B offers the same hand of friendship, to which A can only smile in return. After a moment A offers a foot to B's hand, which B slaps quizzically. She then begins to wander off towards stage right, bemused by this behaviour. Meanwhile, A begins to shuffle in the chair, B hears the noise and looks back at A. At which point A freezes. (This can be done twice for added effect.)

Then, B sees A struggling and returns to where he is sat. B looks closely at A and prods to see if·he is really stuck. Upon discovering that A cannot budge, B breaks into uncontrollable laughter (still in mime, of course!). A's pitiful glance brings B back to the severity of the situation. B pauses to think, suddenly gets inspiration and strikes a pose to show her strength. She then does everything within her power to free A, without touching the chair herself. B starts by pulling a hand, then tries the leg—A shows that this hurts, and when B tries to pull the other leg, A quickly tucks it under the chair out of reach. B then goes behind A, lifts up his elbows and attempts to lift him off the chair, again to no avail.

Finally, B flexes her fingers, grasps A's ears and gives a tug, but still to no avail. B shrugs her shoulders at A and begins to back around the chair, looking for another possible way of freeing A. At this point, B slips on a piece of paper, which she picks up in disgust. As she goes to throw it away she notices some writing—DO NOT TOUCH. After a moment it dawns on her that this must have been a warning sign placed on the chair. She frowns and wags her finger at A, who sheepishly averts his gaze. B thinks again and realizes the necessary solution. She places her hands together, as a sign of prayer, closes her eyes and begins to pray. A remains bemused by this whole action. B soon realizes that A is not paying any attention, so opens her eyes and sweeps her hand past A's eyes in order to make him close them. Then B returns to prayer. A takes the whole thing more seriously now and after a few moments the initial hand is free.

A looks upwards, smiles and begins to pray again more fervently. The second hand quickly becomes free, followed by A almost being sprung backwards out of the chair. He looks himself up and down in amazement, gives a thumbs up to God and taps B on the shoulder. B ignores the tap and carries on praying. A taps harder. B turns away slightly. Finally, A gives B a good shove. B spins round to find out who is pushing her, only to spot A smiling back at her, free from the chair. They give each other a double hand slap and A begins to wander off the stage. B quickly calls him back, pointing to the sign on the floor and gestures towards the chair, suggesting that the sign needs to be put back. They take the sign between them and replace it gingerly on the back of the chair. Turning to the audience they wipe their brows in relief, taking their hands from their foreheads and sweeping down into a bow.

This sketch can be followed by a brief explanation of how we easily fall into the temptation of doing things that don't seem too bad at first but that eventually get us deeper and deeper into trouble. The only way out of our sticky predicament is to call on God.

Drama/Adventure story

The adventures of Sid and Basher: II

Sid felt himself being jerked backwards by the seat of his jeans. He wriggled and squirmed in a vain attempt to free himself.

'No one's going to come to your rescue.' The gruff voice of his captor broke his silent struggle. 'You see, we're right by the ship's engines, and no one's going to hear you shouting for help above this racket. And this cabin's a spare one, so no one ever comes down 'ere. So you may as well give up struggling and behave yourself, you 'orrible little urchin.'

'No way!' thought Sid, and he shouted at the top of his voice, 'HELP! HELP!'

''Elp! 'Elp!', one of the robbers mimicked him in a sarcastic voice. 'Who's going to come and save you? Your granny? I DON'T THINK SO! Now, come here! You're starting to get on my nerves!'

But Sid wasn't taking any notice. His efforts to free himself had started to succeed and he gave just one more enormous wriggle. He felt the man's grasp loosen and he lurched forward, whipping round for all the world like a rugby fly-half and dived between the man's legs. Hands came out in all directions as the robbers tried to catch him for a second time. Sid could hear himself shouting 'HELP! HELP! HELP!' as he scooted around the room. He was starting to think he couldn't go on much longer playing cat and mouse in such a small space.

Then suddenly the door burst open with tremendous force, sending the robber who was blocking it flying across the room. Sid glanced up. . . and there was Basher, come to the rescue! Basher quickly took in the situation and leapt on top of the nearest robber, bringing him neatly to the ground. Basher sat on him.

'Run, Sid! Go on, get going! I heard you call! I knew you needed me! Run! Run!'

Sid took his chance. He ran through the open door and down the corridor as fast as his little legs could carry him. Without looking back he turned into another corridor, and then another.

'Well done, Basher!' he croaked over his shoulder as he gasped for air. 'You're so brave! Fancy you hearing me calling for help, Basher! Basher? Basher?' Sid suddenly realized that he was alone. He stopped running and turned round.

'Basher! Where are you? This is no time for playing hide and seek! Stop playing around, Basher!'

But, except for the distance rumble of the ship's engine, the corridor was silent. Sid called and called, but there was no reply from his friend and rescuer. He started back down the corridor, trying to find his way back to the robber's cabin. But in the maze of corridors he totally lost his bearings. He was getting to the point of giving up all hope of either finding his friend, or anyone else for that matter, when he spotted a sign on one of the doors. CAPTAIN'S CABIN. Sid took a deep breath and knocked timidly on the door.

At once the door flew open.

'Any news?' asked the captain. 'Oh! Who are you, boy? Look, go and play your games somewhere else, I'm very busy!' The captain bent down towards Sid. 'We're trying to find some robbers.' The captain patted Sid on the head.

'But I know where they are!' spluttered Sid.

The captain looked stern. 'That's not funny, young man, this is a serious business. Now, off you go and play your games somewhere else!' And he slammed the door in Sid's face.

Sid's voice drifted helplessly in the air, 'But they're by the engines!' he squeaked. He felt a sob rising in his throat and misting his eyes. It was no good. The captain would never believe a little lad like him! He wandered off, not knowing where he was going, but knowing that he had to find Basher.

At last, turning into yet another corridor he suddenly realized that this was the right one! There at the end was the door to the robbers' cabin. And it was open! Sid caught his breath. He flattened himself against the wall of the corridor and moved cautiously towards the open door. He was a mere two paces away when. . . SPLASH! Sid froze.

'Oh, no,' he gasped, 'they've thrown Basher overboard!' Taking his courage in both hands he peered round the door and. . . YOU'LL HAVE TO WAIT UNTIL TOMORROW TO FIND OUT WHAT HAPPENED!

Drama/Adventure story link

Sid called out for help, even though the robbers said it would do no good. But Basher heard him call and came to the rescue. When we call out to Jesus, he can rescue us—not just when we get into nasty situations, but for the whole of our lives.

Memory verse

Romans 10:13. 'Everyone who calls on the name of the Lord shall be saved.'

A rap: Everyone who calls / on the name of the Lord / shall / be / saved ///
/ = clap

Repeat the memory verse five times, starting off with a normal voice, secondly in a posh voice, next in a really common voice, then in a really quiet voice and finally shout it out as loud as you can. (This highlights in the child's mind that it doesn't matter who you are or what you are like. When the Bible says 'everyone', it really means everyone!)

Quiz

Questions could include:

What do you call a girl standing between two goal posts?
Annette

What do you call a boy with a spade?
Doug

What do you call a girl with a frog on her head?
Lily

What do you call a boy without a spade?
Douglas

Lucy: Hey, Bert, let's play a game.

Bert: OK. What do you want to play?

Lucy: Hide and seek—and I'm going to hide!

Bert: But you always do. . .

Lucy: . . . Just look the other way and count to 10.

Bert: OK. 1. . . 2. . . 3. . . etc.

Lucy: (*Quietly, and out of sight*) Now where shall I hide?. . . Hey, this old suitcase should be just the place. . . The lid's a bit heavy. . . (*Creak!*) There! This is brilliant! He'll never find me here!

Bert: . . . 9. . . 10! Coming! Ready or not! Now, where is she?

Lucy: (*Nervously*) Ooh, it's a bit dark!

Bert: What was that?

Lucy: (*Scared*) Aaagh, I think there's a spider! Bert, where are you?

Bert: Was that Lucy?

Lucy: HELP! The lid's stuck! I'm in the old suitcase, Bert, let me out! HELP!

Bert: It's OK, I'm coming. (*He disappears*) Cor, this lid is stiff. (*Creak*) There you go, Lucy.

Lucy: Oh, thank you, Bert! (*Kiss, kiss!*)

Bert: Euggh! What did you do that for?

Lucy: Well, you saved me. You're my hero!

Bert: Well, I heard you call out for help, Lucy. Come on, everybody's waiting to see if you're OK. (*they both re-appear*)

Lucy: Hey, everyone, Bert's my hero. He saved me!

Bert: Well, it's amazing what can happen when you call out for help, isn't it?

Lucy: Yeah, thank you, Bert. I thought I might never get out of there!

Bert: That's OK, Lucy. But I think that's enough of hide and seek for one day, don't you?

Lucy: If you say so, Bert.

Bert: Come on then. Bye everyone!

Lucy: Bye, bye!

Bible story

Blind Bartimaeus calls out to Jesus for help.
Read the three accounts in Matthew 20:29–34,
Mark 10:46–52 and Luke 18:35–43.

Key points

- *The crowds considered Bartimaeus to be totally unworthy to call out to Jesus.*
- *Bartimaeus knows that he needs Jesus' help and perseveres.*
- *He recognizes who Jesus is, even though he can't see him.*
- *He does not waste his opportunity to meet Jesus.*
- *He responds joyfully when he realizes that Jesus has heard his call.*
- *He is confident that Jesus can heal him.*
- *Jesus rewards Bartimaeus' faith.*
- *Bartimaeus responds to Jesus by following him.*

Style suggestion

Cast: Narrator and two others (A and B)
(A mimes sitting down with hands together in a cup shape, begging)

Narr: *(To audience)* What do you think he's doing? Yes, he's begging. You see, in Bible days if you were blind or deaf you didn't get any money from the government and no one would offer you a job. You had to beg and hope that someone would give you money, otherwise you would go hungry. Beggars were wretched but some people found them a nuisance! Watch. . .

B: *(Mimes a rich person swaggering along the street)*

A: Give me some money. Please! Pretty please. Pretty, pretty please!

B: *(Mimes dropping a single coin into the beggar's hand)* There, that's all you're getting. Now, be off with you!

Narr: No one liked beggars. They tried to avoid them whenever they could! There once was a beggar called Bartimaeus—blind Bartimaeus. Once, he had been able to see, but somehow he had lost his sight. How he longed to be able to see again! He had heard about a man named Jesus who could make blind people see! So imagine how excited he was when he heard that Jesus was coming his way! Bartimaeus started to shout out, trying to attract Jesus' attention.

A: Jesus! Son of David! Take pity on me!

Narr: But the crowd scolded him.

B: *(Irritably)* Be quiet, Bartimaeus. Jesus is a VERY IMPORTANT PERSON!

Narr: But Bartimaeus shouted even louder!

A: Jesus! Son of David! Take pity on me!

Narr: *(To audience)* Now why don't you pretend to be the crowd and tell Bartimaeus to be quiet? All together, after three, shout: 'BE QUIET, BARTIMAEUS!' *(Audience practises this)* That's very good. Now, this time, Bartimaeus is going to try to make his voice heard above you lot. Are you ready? He's going to shout, 'Jesus! Son of David! Take pity on me!' *(B joins in with audience shouting 'Be quiet, Bartimaeus'. A shouts, 'Jesus! Son of David! Take pity on me!')*

Narr: Somehow, Jesus heard Bartimaeus calling him and. . . *(B interrupts)*

B: I say, can someone shut him up? I don't like beggars!

Narr: No! Jesus is asking you to take Bartimaeus to him!

B: Hey, come on you. He's calling you! *(A jumps to his feet)*

Narr: So Bartimaeus threw off his coat, jumped up and went to Jesus. Can you imagine—the very people who had been shouting at Bartimaeus to be quiet now guided him to Jesus! *(B guides A to narrator)*

Narr: And Jesus asked Bartimaeus what he wanted him to do for him.

A: Teacher, I want to see again!

Narr: And Jesus replied, 'Go, your faith has made you well!' And straight away, Bartimaeus could see! *(A dances around crying out, 'I can see, I can see!')* Everyone was amazed! And do you know what Bartimaeus did? He chose to follow Jesus. It doesn't matter if we're rich or poor, we can call Jesus anytime. He always hears us and he calls *us* to follow him.

Quiz 2, memory verse recap, prayer and theme song

The Adventure Cruise

CALL—Blind Bartimaeus calls out for help

We have 5 senses. Can you fit them into the crossword from the clues?

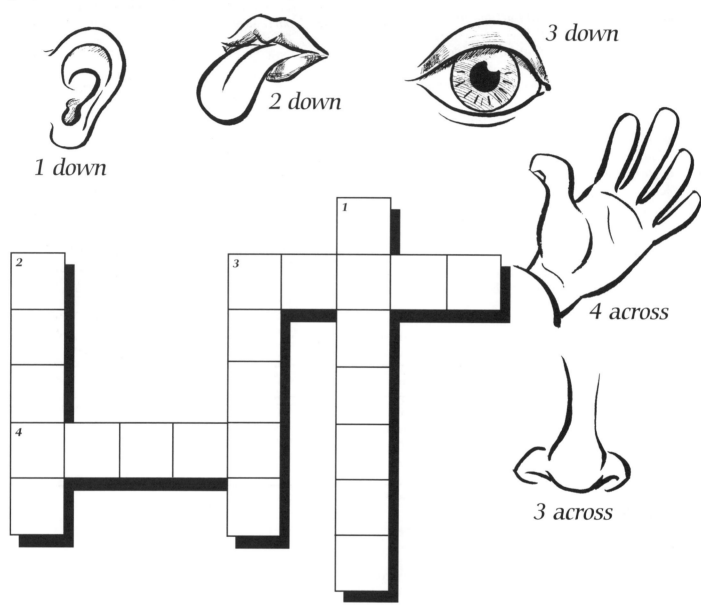

1 down

2 down

3 down

4 across

3 across

 *Which sense didn't Bartimaeus have?* ____

Which sense helps us to listen to God? _____

Which sense can show love to our friends? ____

Colour in today's story

 *Black out every letter with a dot above it to reveal today's memory verse.*

```
e s v e o r a y p j e s ·
o n e w r p h s o e v r ·
m c e a i l s l s s u s ·
o o n f t h b e c r y r ·
n a m e z o f j t h e n ·
l k o r q d u s h a l l
i b e r e s a v e d m e ·
```

Romans 10 verse 13

Day 3
CHANGE

Zacchaeus' life-changing encounter with Jesus

Aim

To show that when we encounter Jesus it is a life-changing experience. This is something that comes from inside and results in changes on the outside.

Warm up

See Day 1

Theme song

See Day 1

Theme illustration

This is a visual illustration that involves two people, a white or black board, or an overhead projector and a rubber or wiper.

Person 1: Did you know that (*name second person*) is an excellent artist and I've asked them to come and draw a car for me.

Person 2: (*Comes up onto stage and starts drawing on the board*)

Person 1: (*Takes no notice of what person 2 is doing*) Can you imagine what life must have been like before cars were invented? Less noise, less pollution, fewer roads, no traffic jams. But long journeys were really difficult. In fact, what we consider to be quite a short distance today, seemed like miles and miles when you had to rely on your own pair of feet to do the walking. . . etc. etc. . .

Person 2: (*Has drawn a house instead of a car*)

Person 1: . . . Look, I didn't ask you to draw me a house! I asked you to draw me a car! Well, never mind. Maybe we could change it into a car. Put some wheels on the bottom corners. . . that's it. Now give it a bonnet. . . and a boot. And wing mirrors. . . and an exhaust. (*To audience*)What else do cars have?

Person 2: (*Draws whatever audience shout out*)

Person 1: There, that looks like a car, doesn't it? What do you mean it doesn't? What do you mean it looks a mess? It looks all right to me! Well, what do we need to do to change it? Rub it out and start again? Well, all right, and this time I'll help you. . .

Person 2: (*Draws a car with the help of audience and person 1*)

Person 1: You know, when we ask him, God rubs out all the things we do wrong and forgives us. Then he helps us put things right and helps us not to make a mess of things. . .

Drama/Adventure story

The adventures of Sid and Basher: III

The cabin was empty, but the window was open! Sid dashed across to the window and looked out. Far below him he could see the deep blue sea with little white waves chopping its surface. And there floating in the water was a bag! A bag of. . . rubbish!

'It's not Basher!' exclaimed Sid. 'They haven't thrown him overboard!' He drew his head back into the cabin and looked around. It looked a mess. Chairs and tables were lying on their sides and there was a broken lamp on the floor. Suddenly Sid spotted a slip of white paper pinned to the back of one of the chairs. Sid's fingers shook as he plucked it off the chair and read the spidery writing scrawled across the sheet: BACK OFF BOY IF YOU EVER WANT TO SEE YOUR FRIEND AGAIN.

Here was the evidence Sid needed! He grasped the note firmly in his hand and rushed out of the room. This time, he found his way back to the captain's cabin quite easily. He knocked loudly and confidently on the closed door. Once again the door was opened quickly and once again he found himself standing in front of the ship's captain.

'I've got proof! I've got proof that they took Basher! Look!' Sid jammed the note under the captain's nose. This time the captain smiled at the boy.

'Yes, son, I know', he said gently.

'What! You mean you've changed your mind? You believe me? You're going to help?' Sid tripped over his questions in his excitement. He couldn't believe that the captain was going to take him seriously.

'Yes, yes, I've changed my mind. I do believe you. You see, I've had a note from the robbers too. It says that they've got your friend, Basher, and they'll dump him overboard if I don't get a helicopter for them. There's nothing I can do to make them change their minds. The helicopter's on its way.'

Sid couldn't believe his ears! 'What! You're going to let them get away with it? And what about Basher? How do you know they won't harm him anyway?'

But Sid's questions were drowned by the whirring of a loud engine, coming closer and closer. Sid paused for a split second and then ran as fast as he could towards the staircase which led up to the ship's deck. The helicopter was hovering over the ship, its rope ladder trailing from its open door.

Suddenly the captain was behind Sid and there, coming around the side of the deck, were the robbers. The one who had caught hold of Sid in the cabin was carrying a large, heavy-looking sack over his shoulder.

Sid started to run towards the robbers. 'You can't let them get away!' he shouted to the captain, 'They've got Basher!'

The robbers started to run towards the helicopter's rope ladder as it swung above the deck. Sid wasn't fast enough for them and soon they were climbing up the ladder and disappearing inside the helicopter.

'Stop! Stop! Come back with Basher!' Sid yelled at the top of his voice. The robber who was carrying the sack was running towards the rope ladder, struggling with the weight of the sack as he grasped hold of the ladder's bottom rung. Sid leapt after him and grabbed hold of the sack.

'It's all right, Basher, I won't let them take you!' He gasped. The robber was forced to let go of the sack as he scrambled to make his escape. As the sack dropped to the ground Sid opened it up and. . . YOU'LL HAVE TO WAIT UNTIL TOMORROW TO FIND OUT WHAT HAPPENED!

Drama/Adventure story link

The captain changed his mind when he heard from the robbers and it made all the difference. When Sid came back the captain treated him much better. We change too when we ask Jesus to be our friend—not all at once, but gradually he helps us to make the right choices and try to live a better life.

Memory verse

2 Corinthians 5:17 'When anyone is joined to Christ he is a new creation, the old has gone and the new has come.'

A song: The sheet music can be found in Appendix B on page 146. The song can be found on the *Ultimate Holiday Club Guide* cassette, available from your local Christian bookshop, or, in case of difficulty, direct from BRF.

Quiz

Questions could include:

What do you get if you swallow a £5 note?
   No change.

How do you change a cow?
   Turn it into a field.

Why can't Hannah change?
   Because she'll always be the same, whichever way you look at it.

Why did the captain change his mind?
   Because he had a note from the robbers too.

Puppets

Lucy: Hi, Bert.

Bert: Hi, Lucy.

Lucy: (*Whispers*) Pssst. . . You're not still wearing that horrible smelly red jumper, are you?

Bert: What do you mean? This is my favourite jumper!

Lucy: But we're learning about change today, so the least you could do is to change your jumper!

Bert: Lucy, don't be silly! That's not the sort of change we're talking about!

Lucy: It's not? Well, what else can it mean then?

Bert: It means a much bigger change than just changing your clothes.

Lucy: Oh yeah, clever clogs, like what?

Bert: A change on the inside!

Lucy: Yuck! Like a tummy transplant, do you mean?

Bert: No, silly! More of a change of heart.

Lucy: Whaaat!!

Bert: It means you change from doing the things you know are wrong to doing the things you know are right.

Lucy: Oh, I see. That's difficult though, isn't it!

Bert: Yes, so you need to listen carefully and then you'll know how to do it.

Lucy: Right!

Bert: Say good-bye then, Lucy.

Lucy: Good-bye then, Lucy!

Bert: Come on, Lucy. Bye, bye everyone. . . (*They disappear*)

Lucy: Bert, are you going to change that jumper or not? Bert? Bert!

Bible story

Zacchaeus' life-changing encounter with Jesus.
Read Luke's account in chapter 19:1–10.

Key points

- *Zacchaeus had found a nice little niche for himself in life which made him very rich.*
- *He was resourceful—he didn't let the crowd stop him doing what he wanted.*
- *He was drawn to Jesus through curiosity rather than because he wanted his help.*
- *He joyfully responded to Jesus' authority (I must stay in your house today)*
- *When Zacchaeus met Jesus his life was immediately and spectacularly changed.*
- *Everyone—except Jesus—had thought that Zacchaeus was beyond the pale.*
- *Jesus does not give us up as lost; he takes every possible step to save us.*

Style suggestion

Cast: Narrator and two others (A and B)

Narr: He had a lot of money!

A: In fact, he had lots and lots of money!

B: In fact he had LOADS of money! Loads 'n' loads 'n' loads 'n' loads. . . (*other two give him the dead eye*). . . of money. . . oops!

Narr: Yep! He was very rich!

B: Yep! He was very, very, very, very. . . (*other two give him that look again*). . . rich!

Narr: He had many friends.

B: Yep! Loads 'n' loads 'n' loads. . . hang on, he didn't have any friends!

Narr: What do you mean, he didn't have any friends? Of course he had friends! He was very rich!

A: Yeah! All rich people have friends!

B: That's not true! There are a lot of lonely rich people—money doesn't make you happy, (*To audience*) does it? (*Audience responds*)

B: In fact, they all hated him!

Narr: How do you know?

A: Yeah! How do you know?

B: Because he was a tax collector. That means he collected everyone's money and gave it to the Roman government. Everyone hated the Romans, so they hated tax collectors too!

Narr: So he hadn't won the lottery, then?

B: No, he was mean!

A: Very mean!

B: Very, very, very, very. . . mean! But he was probably very lonely, too.

Narr: Jesus was in Jericho.

A: Everyone wanted to see him!

B: Even our friend the tax collector!

A: Zacchaeus!

Narr: There was a large crowd.

A: A very large crowd!

B: A very, very, very, very. . . (*others give him that look again*). . . large crowd.

Narr: Have you ever been in a large crowd when you just couldn't see over their heads?

A: Maybe people let you through to the front, or people lifted you up so you could see!

B: Zacchaeus couldn't see! (*He walks round to the back of the other two and strains his neck, trying to see over their heads*)

Narr: (*To A*) Hey, look! It's Zacchaeus the tax collector!

A: Don't let him through! We hate tax collectors! (*B runs to left, but is blocked by other two, runs to right and is blocked. He tries to lift himself up on their shoulders, run through their legs etc., but they continue to block him.*)

Narr: There was no way they would let him through.

A: So he ran off up the road. (*B mimes running*) And climbed a tree!

Narr: A tree!

A: Have you ever seen a rich man in a suit, trying to climb a tree! Well, he was up in a flash!

Narr: Very flash!

B: (*Climbs onto a chair and mimes looking down the road*)

Narr: Eventually he could see Jesus and the crowd coming down the road.

A: He could see the crowd, but they couldn't see him!

Narr: Then suddenly Jesus stopped right underneath Zacchaeus' tree, looked up into the branches and said. . .

A: Hurry down, Zacchaeus, for I must stay in your house today.

Narr: So Zacchaeus scrambled down from the tree. (*B climbs down from chair, looking smug*)

B: This way! (*Goes off stage*)

Narr: So off Zacchaeus and Jesus went. Imagine how much the rest of the crowd moaned!

A: Why Zacchaeus? He's just a cheat. He's a tax collector!

Narr: Moan, moan, moan. It's not fair!

A: But no one else had ever been kind to Zacchaeus, or wanted to go to his house.

Narr: After a little while Zacchaeus came back, and he had CHANGED!

B: (*Comes back and mimes giving money to everyone*)

A: He *has* changed! He's started giving money away!

Narr: Jesus said. . .

A: The Son of Man came to seek and to save the lost.

B: Yep! Even mean, greedy cheats can change! Jesus has time for everyone and he loves even me!

Narr and A: Especially you!

Quiz 2, memory verse recap, prayer and theme song

The Adventure Cruise

CHANGE—Zacchaeus' life-changing encounter with Jesus

Find and circle the 10 changes in the pictures of Zacchaeus and then colour in the pictures.

How many words can you make out of

ZACCHAEUS

Today's memory verse has been blown off course! Can you rearrange the words back in to the correct order?

joined when has is Christ old anyone is creation, a is to the and come has he the new gone

2 Corinthians 5 verse 1

Cross out the wrong answers.

Zacchaeus was a...farmer/doctor/tax collector/fisherman

Zacchaeus wanted to see...David/Peter/Jesus/Paul

Zacchaeus was very...tall/thin/fat/short

Zacchaeus...jumped up and down/climbed a tree/ran away/knelt down

Zacchaeus showed he had changed by...buying a new coat/giving back some of the money he had taken from people /giving back 4 times as much money as he had taken from people

Day 4
COMMITMENT

The paralysed man and his four committed friends

Aim

To show that the Christian life is not always easy and that we need to remain committed to God—just as he is to us. Also, we don't face life on our own, and we should help each other along the way.

Warm up

See Day 1

Theme song

See Day 1

Theme illustration 1
The Commitment Sketch

Cast: Narrator, Mate 1 (Male), Mate 2 (Female)

Narr: Mate 1 and Mate 2 are best mates

Mate 1: Hi! How are you doing? (*Turns to audience*) We're the bestest mates!

Mate 2: We're the coolest mates!

Mate 1: We are check mates!

Mate 2: That's chess, silly! We are. . . coffee mates!

Mate 1: That's coffee, silly!

Mate 2: Well, there's a big word beginning with 'C'. . . we're. . .

Mate 1: Cornflakes!

Mate 2: Do I look like a cornflake?

Mate 1: Um. . . er. . .

Mate 2: Ah! I know it! We're COMMITTED mates!

Mate 1: Yeah! Committed mates!. . . what's that mean?

Mate 2: Er. . . I don't know! Let's ask somebody brainy. . . Ah (*Narrator*) will do!

(*Mates whistle*)

Narr: Do you want me for something?

Mate 1: What does committed mean?

Narr: What, when you're best mates like you two?

Both: Yeah!

Narr: It means you always help each other.

Mate 2: Come on, Granddad (*Helps Mate 1 walk*)

Mate 1: I'm coming, dear. . . ooooh! (*They giggle*)

Narr: You stand by each other, whatever.

Mate 1: Can't get much closer! (*They stand back to back*)

Narr: You support each other. (*Mate 1 lifts Mate 2 onto back*) Steady now! You might play football together. (*Mates do can-can*) What's that?

Mate 1: I was kicking the can!

Narr: And very importantly, you must always stick together.

Both: Aah! Help! We're stuck! Oh dear, we're stuck!

Narr: No, no! I mean you stick up for each other.

Both: Oi! Don't you pick on my mate! (*Pointing into mid-air*)

Mate 2: Marmite? That's what you put on toast! (*Mimes spreading over hand*)

Mate 1: No! My *mate*!

Mate 2: Oh! My mate marmite!

Narr: (*To audience*) Are they best mates? (*Audience responds*) But one day something happened. . . (*Both mates bump each other away*)

Mate 2: Get away you! (*They quarrel with one another*)

Mate 1: I don't want to be your friend anyway!

Mate 2: That's fine by me! (*They pull faces and stamp feet. Then freeze poses*)

Narr: (*To audience*) Are they best mates now? (*Audience responds*) This is how it all started. . .

Mate 2: I've got a great idea!

Mate 1: That's not like you!

Mate 2: Let's go to the cinema!

Mate 1: Oh yeah?

Mate 2: There's this really exciting, action-packed, mega film. . .

Mate 1: What's that, then?

Mate 2: *The Little Mermaid!*

Mate 1: Great! er. . . yeah!

Mate 2: I'll meet you at. . . (*Both look at watches*) a quarter past seven at the back of the school, OK? See you then. (*She walks away*)

Mate 1: OK, half past seven at the front of the school. See ya. (*He walks in opposite direction. They both freeze at edge of stage for a few seconds, then creep around audience, backing up to each other.*)

Mate 1: Where is she?

Mate 2: He's late!

Both: I'm sick of waiting. (*They bump into each other*)

Mate 1: Oh, it's you. . .

Mate 2: Where do you think you've been?

Mate 1: Where've I been! What about you!? (*They start to argue*)

Mate 2: I don't want to be your friend anyway.

Mate 1: That's fine by me! (*They pull faces and stamp feet. Then freeze poses*)

Narr: Are they best mates now? (*Audience responds*) Now, what could they have said to each other to stay best mates? (*Audience responds*) Well, let's rewind and try again. . . (*Mates rewind poses*)

Mate 1: Oh, it's you. . .

Mate 2: Where do you think you've been?

Mate 1: Where've I been! What about you!?

Mate 2: I thought we agreed to meet at. . .

Both: (*Mate 2*) a quarter past seven at the back of the school. (*Mate 1*) half past seven at the front of the school. (*They start quarrel and then quieten down and shy away as they realize their mistake.*)

Mate 2: (*Softly*) You got it wrong. . .

Mate 1: No. . . you got it wrong!

Both: Yeah, um. . . we both got it wrong. . .

Mate 2: S. . . s. . . s. . .

Mate 1: S. . . s. . . sausages.

Mate 2: S. . . s. . . sugarlumps.

Mate 1: S. . . s. . . school dinners.

Mate 2: Yeuck! S. . . s. . . sorry. (*Sheepish*)

Mate 1: Yeah! Sorry. Um. . . best mates?

Mate 2: (*Thinks a bit*) Yeah! (*Hand slap*) Let's go and see that action-packed mega film. (*To audience*) What was it? (*Audience responds*)

Narr: Well, that's better! But where did the problem begin? Let's have an action replay and find out. . .

Mate 2: I've got a great idea!

Mate 1: That's not like you!

Mate 2: Let's go to the cinema!

Mate 1: Oh yeah?

Mate 2: There's this really exciting, action-packed, mega film. . .

Mate 1: What's that, then?

Mate 2: The Little Mermaid!

Mate 1: Great! er. . . yeah!

Mate 2: I'll meet you at. . . (*both look at watches*) a quarter past seven at the back of the school, OK?

Mate 1: Ok, half past seven at the front of the school. See ya. (*He goes to walk off*)

Mate 2: Hey, hang on a moment! What did you say?

Mate 1: Um. . .

Mate 2: Read my lips.

Mate 1: Got no writing on.

Mate 2: Watch my lips. (*Gets closer*) Yeuck! You nearly kissed me then! (*Emphasizes slowly*) A—quarter—past—seven—at—the—back—of—the—school!

Mate 1: But if we meet at *half* past seven, we'll still be in plenty of time. And if we meet at the *front* of the school we won't have so far to go!

Mate 2: Wait a minute, I'm getting all defused!

Mate 1: Confused.

Mate 2: Sorry, I get trouble with my worms!

Mate 1: Words!

Mate 2: Oh yeah! So, it's half past seven at the front of the school. (*To audience*) What is it? (*Audience repeats. Mates walk away from each other and freeze on edge of stage*)

(*Mates start to move towards each other back to back*)

Mate 1: It's half past seven.

Mate 2: It's half past seven.

Mate 1: Here I am at the front of the school.

Mate 2: Here I am at the front of the school.

Mate 1: I wonder if she'll be there?

Mate 2: I wonder if he'll be there?

Mate 1: I hope so!

Mate 2: I hope so!

(*Mates bump into each other*)

Both: Hi!

Mate 1: Well, here we are!

Mate 2: Let's go and see that mega film! (*To audience*) What is it? (*Audience responds*) Yeah! *The Little Mermaid!*

Both: Bye! (*They run off together excitedly*)

Theme illustration 2
Co-OPeraTionS

Split your group into teams of four. Give each team member a card with a letter on. The four letters given to each team are: O P T S. As the teams hear a word in the story which uses these four letters they quickly have to make their letters into the correct word. As soon as they have spelt the word they hold up their cards in the correct order. You will need a judge to decide which team was first each time, and which team is the overall winner.

The story

We once had a dog called SPOT. One day I took him for a walk. Suddenly he saw a cat and he ran towards the road.

'STOP!', I shouted! 'SPOT! STOP!' And he did. We carried on with our walk. We went into the park and there I saw my friends playing with some spinning TOPS. SPOT ran up to them and picked up one of the TOPS in his mouth.

'Drop the top, SPOT!' I shouted to him, 'Why do you always have to put things in your mouth? Now look what you've done—they've got soggy spinning TOPS!'

When we got home SPOT saw my mum in the garden and ran to meet her. He wagged his tail so hard that he knocked all her flower POTS off the garden wall.

'Oh, SPOT' my POTS!' said my mum, 'Don't you ever STOP! Look at all those broken flower POTS!'.

But SPOT wasn't listening. He'd spotted the POSTman at the top of the path. The POSTman spotted SPOT. He quickly hopped over the gate and made a hasty retreat, leaving the POST on the path. He didn't STOP to see what SPOT was up to. SPOT picked up the POST in his mouth.

'SPOT', I called, 'Drop!' SPOT dropped the soggy POST by the broken POTS. What a mess! It's a good job we love you, SPOT!

Theme illustration 3
Skiing

You will need to prepare a pair of three-foot planks for each team. Each plank will need to be drilled and have rope tied through to form hand grips for the teams to hold on to as they walk. Have enough volunteers for two teams of three. Each team will need to co-ordinate their actions, moving their legs together in order to

'ski' from one point to another. This is a good link into the Bible story, showing what we can achieve when we work together as a team.

Drama/Adventure story

The adventures of Sid and Basher: IV

As the last robber disappeared up the rope ladder, Sid's attention was drawn to something much more important. For a split second he forgot the robbers as he looked into the sack. It was full of glittering, sparkling, dazzling, shimmering jewels. Sid leapt to his feet and looked up to where the last of the robbers was

just climbing into the helicopter.

'Where's Basher?' he shouted. 'What have you done with my friend?'

''e's stored away— work it out for yourself!' the robber sneered back at him.

Sid didn't wait to answer back. Finding Basher was the most important thing on his mind! He ran back down the stairs and along the corridor.

'Basher! Basher! Where are you?' he yelled at the top of his voice. He pushed open cabin doors to his left and his right as he ran. People started to come out of their cabins to see what all the shouting was about. He pushed through them and ran blindly on, calling and calling for his friend.

Suddenly Sid found himself in front of a door marked STORES. KEEP OUT. Sid pushed hard on the door and it flew open.

'Basher?' he yelled. There was a muffled answer from inside a large trunk standing at the back of the room. 'Basher?' he called again. Once again Sid heard a muffled response, this time followed by a soft thudding sound which seemed to come from inside the trunk.

Sid ran forward and turned the key which was sitting in the lock on the front of the chest. He pushed up the heavy lid and peered inside.

And there was Basher! Safe and sound but firmly gagged and bound. Sid untied his friend and threw his arms around his neck in his relief at seeing him again.

'Yuck! Get off! We've got to find the captain!' yelled Basher. 'Have I got news for him!'

'Basher', said Sid, weakly, 'the captain knows. I've managed to rescue the jewels, but the robbers have got away!'

'Oh, no they haven't!', grinned Basher. 'I managed to give them the slip just long enough to make a quick phone call to the police. They are in the helicopter and will be arresting the robbers as they climb aboard!'

'Basher, you're a hero!' cried Sid.

Just at that moment the captain appeared in the doorway, closely followed by Sid's gran. The captain was delighted. Basher was safe, the robbers had been arrested and the jewellery had been returned to its rightful owners. 'Thanks to you two everything has turned out right', the captain beamed at them, 'I don't know how to thank you. . . but for starters I'm giving you two as well as your grandmother a free cruise. You and your Gran are invited to be my guests of honour as my special guests at the captain's table!'

And he made sure that Sid and Basher had the best holiday ever. THE END.

Drama/Adventure story link

So it worked out all right in the end—but only because Sid and Basher's friendship meant that they were committed to each other. They stuck by each other and helped each other out, right to the end. When we ask Jesus to be our friend he never leaves us and is totally committed to us. So we need to do the same for him, and be committed to what the Bible teaches us, and help our friends, too.

Memory verse

1 John 4:21 'All who love God must also love their brother and their sister.'

A song: The sheet music can be found in Appendix B on page 146. The song can be found on the *Ultimate Holiday Club Guide* cassette, available from your local Christian bookshop, or in case of difficulty, direct from BRF.

Quiz

Questions could include:

Where was Basher?
In the trunk.

Which film did the mates go to see?
The Little Mermaid

Where did the mates eventually meet up?
In front of the school

When did they meet?
Half past seven

What makes light work?
Many hands or electricity!

Bert: Hi Lucy!
Lucy: I'm not talking to you.
Bert: What! Why not?

Lucy: 'Cos I don't want to be your friend anymore.
Bert: (*surprised*) Why not! What have I done?
Lucy: 'Cos you were horrible to me.
Bert: I was horrible to you! When?
Lucy: Yesterday at school.
Bert: I don't remember!
Lucy: In the playground.
Bert: Well, what happened?
Lucy: Well, I was playing football, and I was just about to score a goal. . . when I tripped over and cut my knee really badly. (Sob!)
Bert: Oh, I'm sorry, Lucy. . . but what's that got to do with me?
Lucy: Well, I screamed out for help when I saw you, but you ran off in the other direction. (Sob! sob!)
Bert: Hang on a minute. Was this at the end of playtime?
Lucy: Yee..es. . .
Bert: I remember—I was late for Miss Need's class and I had to hand my homework in. I heard you shout and looked across, but there was a huge crowd of people trying to help you, so I didn't think you needed me.
Lucy: Of course I needed you! You're my best friend!
Bert: I'm sorry, Lucy, I didn't realize it meant that much to you. I promise if it ever happens again, I'll be there to help you.
Lucy: You promise?
Bert: Yes, that's what friends are for—to be committed to each other.
Lucy: Does that mean that they help each other, Bert?
Bert: Yes, Lucy, it does.
Lucy: Oh good! Come on then Bert, let's go and play! Bye bye everyone!
Bert: Bye, bye. . .

Bible Story

The four friends were committed to bringing their paralysed friend to meet Jesus. Read the three accounts in Matthew 9:1–8, Mark 2:1–12 and Luke 5:17–26.

Key Points

● *The four friends wouldn't be put off getting their friend to Jesus by the obstacles in their way.*

● *The four friends worked out a way to get their friend to Jesus. It was a difficult route, but they were determined.*

● *The four friends' plan would not have been possible if they had not all been committed to it.*

- *The paralysed man relied on his friends to help him.*
- *The four friends were committed unselfishly to help the paralysed man without thought of any gain for themselves.*
- *The four friends were confident that their commitment to their friend would be met by Jesus' ability to help him.*

Style suggestion

Cast: Narrator and two others (A and B)

Narr: There was once a man who was paralysed.

B: What, you mean he couldn't move?

Narr: Yes, he could only lie there on his bed all day.

A: But Jesus was in town. . .

B: And he had just healed a man!

A: (*To B*) If he could heal that man, then maybe he could heal our friend!

B: Yeah! We're going to get him to Jesus!

Narr: So they picked up their friend who was lying on his bed—not a bunk bed!—a sort of thin mattress, and they started to carry their friend to Jesus. (*A and B mime picking up their friend on his mattress and stagger along with him, miming chatter and looking very cheerful and hopeful.*)

Narr: Then they stopped and their mouths dropped open. (*A and B's mouths drop open*) You see, there was such a crowd!

A: A massive crowd!

B: Loads 'n' loads 'n' loads 'n' loads of people!

Narr: But they didn't give up.

A: No way! Come on, lads! (*They mime pushing their way through the crowd, standing on feet, elbowing etc.*) Aw, this is a real struggle!

Narr: They made it to the house, but there was no way in! The crowd was tightly packed around the door and windows! Then they had an idea!

B: I've got an idea! Come on!

A: Where're we going?

B: This way!

A: Which way?

B: This way!

Narr: In that country the houses are built with steps on the outside and they lead up onto a flat roof. The friends (there were really four of them) carried the paralysed man up the narrow steps. . .

A: Left a bit. Right a bit. . .

B: Watch out, you nearly pushed me over the edge then!

Narr: . . . and eventually, they found themselves on the flat roof.

A: Oh great! We're up here on this flat roof and Jesus is down below in the house. That really was a great idea!

B: Well, we'll make a hole! Loads of fun! (*He mimes scratching away at the mud roof*)

Narr: So that is what they did! Can you imagine how that hole grew! First they made a small hole. . .

A: (*Squints eye as if looking through a small hole*) Peep bo!

Narr: Then they made the hole bigger. . .

B: Look, there he is!

Narr: . . . and bigger and bigger. Until eventually they were able to peer over the edge and look down on Jesus and the people in the house—who were brushing mud out of their hair and off their robes. (*He mimes brushing off the mud.*)

A and B: (*Mime looking down and waving*) Hi!

Narr: And they lowered their friend down to Jesus.

A and B: All together now, lads. Careful there! (*They mime lowering friend down*)

Narr: When Jesus saw what the four friends had done he said something really strange. He looked at the man lying on his mattress and he said, 'Your sins are forgiven, my friend.' Some of the people in the crowd were thinking to themselves. . .

A: Only God can forgive sins!

B: Who does he think he is?

Narr: But Jesus knew what they were thinking and asked. . .

A: Is it easier to say, 'Your sins are forgiven you', or to say, 'Get up and walk?' I will prove to you that the Son of Man has authority on earth to forgive sins.

B: (*Lies at narrator's feet*)

Narr: He said to the paralysed man. . .

A: Get up, pick up your bed, and go home!

B: (*Starts to get up slowly and gingerly*)

Narr: He found he had strength in his arms and legs and his body, and he got up!

B: (*Gets up slowly, but then suddenly dances round*) I can walk! I can walk!

Narr: The friends had worked together as a team. They never gave up, even though it was such hard work!

A and B: Yep! We had to get our hands dirty!

Narr: But they were overjoyed to see what Jesus had done for their friend.

A: It wasn't easy!

B: It was difficult!

A: But it was exciting!

B: It was a pleasure!

Quiz 2, memory verse recap, prayer and theme song

The Adventure Cruise

COMMITMENT—*The paralysed man and his four committed friends*

Colour in this picture of the four friends as they help the paralysed man get to Jesus

Help the four friends to find the house where Jesus was.

Turn the clues around and put them in the right place in the crossword.

Across

3. suseJ
5. nevigrof
6. nos
8. seesirahP
10. klaw
11. laeh
13. nam

Down

1. droL
2. nem
3. melasureJ
4. snis
7. yaw
8. rewop
9. htiaf
12. yal

 Unscamble today's memory verse.

___ ___ ____ ___ ____ ____ ____ _____ _____ ___ _____
lal how elvo dGo stum salo vole herit rotherb dan ersits

1 John 4 verse 21

 **What were the four friends?** _____

How can we be committed to our friends? _____

How can we be committed to Jesus? _____

Write your answers on the lines or draw a picture in the space below.

Day 5
COST

The rich young man finds the cost of following Jesus too great

Aim
To show that if we truly want to follow Jesus we must be prepared to do whatever he asks of us. It is not a decision to be made lightly, but we need to weigh up how much it will really mean to us.

Warm up
See Day 1

Theme Song
See Day 1

Theme illustration 1
Invite a leader onto the stage and ask them to list the ten commandments. Give them a 'glitzy' prize for every one they get right. After they have completed as many as they can (hopefully all ten!) congratulate them and point out how much better off they are with all the prizes they have won due to their brilliant knowledge of the ten commandments. Then produce an envelope from your pocket and ask if they would like to swap the unknown envelope for all the lovely goodies they have won. (*Get the audience to join in here*). The primed leader refuses to take the envelope and finally walks off stage with all the goodies. Open the envelope pull out a blank cheque. Read out the following words, which are written on the back of the cheque: 'Everyone who leaves (everything) for my sake will receive a hundred times more and will be given eternal life.'

Theme illustration 2
'Count the Cost'
(based on Luke 14:28–33)
Cast: Narrator. Voice 1 & Voice 2

Narr:

If you want to be free, if you want to be right,

Then why not follow Jesus Christ?

But hang on first we've got a tale to tell,

about some folks who didn't do very well.

Voice 1:

I've got some bricks, got some clay.

I think I'll build a house today.

It won't take long, it'll be so neat.

It'll be the best house in all the street.

Voice 2:

Come on lads, it's dark tonight,

Let's go down town and start a fight!

That gang think they're really cute,

But watch them run when they see my boot!

Narr:

So far so good, or so it seems,

but they've made mistakes with their hasty schemes.

I think there's something slightly wrong,

I've never seen them with their faces so long.

Voice 1:

It's almost done, but it isn't funny,

it seems we've run right out of money.

The neigbours think we're really daft,

with half a house there'll be a draught!

Voice 2:

Our gang fought well, but they had more,

I've got two black eyes and a broken jaw.

No one thinks I'm really smart,

I wished I'd planned before the start!

Narr:

So count the cost, it takes a lot.

To follow Jesus means all you've got.

You need to stand against the tide;

Following Jesus is no easy ride.

In any race the prize is there,

But if you want to win, you'll need to prepare.

You need to go against the tide,

this way of life is no easy ride,

You need to be strong, you need to stand,

I'll go with Jesus, and we'll win the land!

Drama/Adventure story

The adventures of Sid and Basher: V

Phew! What an adventure Sid and Basher had! Do you remember how there was a burglary aboard the luxury cruise liner? When Sid got caught he was left with a tricky choice and when he decided to try and get away he didn't quite make it! But when he called out for help, Basher heard his cry and came to the rescue. Basher helped Sid get free, but got caught himself in the process. Sid then had to try to rescue Basher, but when he asked the captain for help he just got pushed to one side. The captain changed his mind, though, when he heard from the robbers himself. From then on Sid proved his commitment to Basher by not giving up the search until he found him. The friends stuck together right through the adventure, to the very end.

Life is quite an adventure at times—maybe not quite like the one Sid and Basher had—but in other ways. We must choose whether or not to follow Jesus. We know that when we do call out to him he will hear us. Then as his friends, he will help us. When we are his friends we gradually change and become more like him. This doesn't happen all at once and we need to remain committed to him, and to each other. Following Jesus is an important choice and we must weigh up the cost involved carefully, to make sure we are prepared to be fully committed.

Memory verse

Matthew 16:24 'If anyone wants to come with me, he must forget self, carry his cross, and follow me.'

A song: The sheet music can be found in Appendix B on page 146. The song can be found on the *Ultimate Holdiay Club Guide* cassette, available from your local Christian bookshop, or, in case of difficulty, direct from BRF.

Quiz

Questions could include:

How do you get four elephants in a mini?
Two in the front, two in the back

How do you get two whales in a mini?
Over the Severn Bridge

How much does it cost to follow Jesus?
Nothing, but it costs everything

Puppets

Bert: What's wrong, Lucy?

Lucy: I don't feel very well—I've got a funny tummy.

Bert: Well, what did you have for breakfast?

Lucy: Nothing.

Bert: That's not like you! You must be ill!

Lucy: I told you so.

Bert: Well, what did you eat last night?

Lucy: Um. . .

Bert: Hang on, wasn't last night your friend's birthday party?

Lucy: Yes, that's right.

Bert: Ah, so it must have been something you ate there?

Lucy: M. . . m. . . maybe. . .

Bert: Tell us what happened, Lucy.

Lucy: Well, we each had to bring something to eat and share. So my mum baked a MASSIVE chocolate cake.

Bert: Cor, yummy!

Lucy: Yeah! I love chocolate cake! Anyway, I put it on the dining room table and then the games started in the lounge.

Bert: Oh great—what did you play?

Lucy: Um. . . I don't know—I stayed behind.

Bert: Why?

Lucy: I thought that maybe I should test the cake.

Bert: What do you mean 'test the cake'?

Lucy: Well, I had a slice, to make sure it was OK.

Bert: And was it?

Lucy: Oh yes, it was really yummy.

Bert: So what happened next?

Lucy: Well, as the others were still playing games, I thought maybe I'd have another bit.

Bert: Another bit?

Lucy: . . . and another bit!

Bert: Lucy—how much of that cake did you eat?

Lucy: (*very quietly*) Er. . . all of it.

Bert: Pardon?

Lucy: All of it.

Bert: You ate all of it. . .

Lucy: Um. . . yes.

Bert: . . . while everyone else was playing games?

Lucy: Yes. It did sound like they were having a good time.

Bert: So you ate the whole cake and now you have a tummy-ache?

Lucy: Yes. I don't know why.

Bert: (*to audience*) I think we do, don't we!

Lucy: Why?

Bert: Lucy, you should have known that eating all that cake would make you sick.

Lucy: I suppose so, but it was so nice. I really don't feel too good, Bert.

Bert: Come on, Lucy, let's get you a glass of water. Bye everyone.

Lucy: Bye, bye—and thank you, Bert.

Bible story

This is the story of the rich young man for whom the cost was to high. Read the accounts in Matthew 19:16–30, Mark 10:17–31 and Luke 18:18–30.

Key points

● *The young man probably always had what he wanted.*

● *He wanted some good value 'life assurance' from Jesus.*

● *Jesus' response took him by surprise.*

● *Sadly, his heart was set on his money, rather than on what Jesus wanted.*

● *If we truly want to follow Jesus we must be prepared to do whatever he asks.*

Style suggestion

Cast: Narrator and two others (A and B)

Narr: There was a young man!

A: Hard working!

B: Ambitious!

Narr: Perhaps a bit pushy!

A: But he knew what he wanted!

B: And he got it!

A and B: (*Sing*) Money, money, money, loads of money!

Narr: If he had lived today he would have had a flashy car. . .

A: Latest computer.

B: Flashy clothes.

Narr: But he didn't! He lived in Jesus' time.

A: In fact, he actually met Jesus!

B: In fact, he actually spoke to Jesus and asked him a question. . .

Narr: He said. . .

A: Good teacher, what must I do to receive eternal life?

Narr: Why do you call me good? No one is good except God alone.

A: (*Shuffles feet*) Yes, well. . .

Narr: You know the commandments: Do not commit adultery. . .

A: I don't!

Narr: . . . do not commit murder. . .

A: I don't!

Narr: . . . do not steal. . .

A: I don't!

Narr: . . . do not accuse anyone falsely. . .

A: I don't!

Narr: . . . respect your father and your mother. . .

A: I don't. . . I mean, I do!

B: Ever since he was a young man he's obeyed all these commandments! (*A looks proud*)

Narr: Then Jesus looked him straight in the eye and said. . .

B: There is still one thing you need to do.

Narr: Sell all you have and give the money to the poor, and you will have riches in heaven; then come and follow me.

A: (*Looks shocked*) What!

B: He said sell all you have and give the money to the poor.

A: (*To audience*) I think I'm going deaf. I thought he said sell all you have and give your money to the poor!

B: He did.

A: He did?

B: Yep.

A: What everything?

B: (*To narrator*) What everything?

Narr: Yes, everything.

B: But he's very rich!

A: I'm very, very rich!

B: He's very, very, very, very, very, very. . .

A: rich!

Narr: I know.

A and B: You know!

Narr: Yes, I know you're very rich. But what's more important to you, your money or me?

A: (*Hangs his head and slowly walks off stage*)

Narr: You see, Jesus knew that that young man's money was very important to him. More important than anything.

B: So did he?

Narr: Did he what?

B: Did he sell everything he had?

Narr: No! This is a sad story. He couldn't do it. He money was too important to him and for him the cost of following Jesus was too high.

B: He turned his back and walked away from Jesus?

Narr: Yep!

B: But the man with the horrible skin disease and Bartimaeus and Zacchaeus and the paralysed man turned to Jesus didn't they?

Narr: Yes they did and their stories had happy endings. But this rich young man didn't and he walked away sad.

Quiz 2, memory verse recap, prayer and theme song

Drama workshop/Crafts display

You may wish to consider an alternative to the previous day's system of rotation. This could give you space to prepare material for a Family Service, hold a drama workshop, or create a special craft display.

The Adventure Cruise

COST—The rich young man finds the cost of following Jesus too great

What does the memory verse say?

If any 1 w 🐜🐜 2 come Y're th me , he must 4get self , 🚗...ry his ✗ ✋ follow me !

Matthew 16 verse 24

Help the rich young man to find his way to Jesus.

POSH HOUSE

FLASH CAR

CASH POINT

LOADS OF MONEY

JESUS

Can you find the words on the wordsearch?

```
p m e f o l l o w o r d
c o m m a n d m e n t s
t n o r o o p a v z w b
J e s u s c o n i c o e
x y z o e v n d g v p f
s t e a l m a t t h e i
a b d f l e t e r n a l
```

come poor sell follow money commandments Jesus steal eternal life

Colour the picture of the rich young man as he walks sadly
away from Jesus.

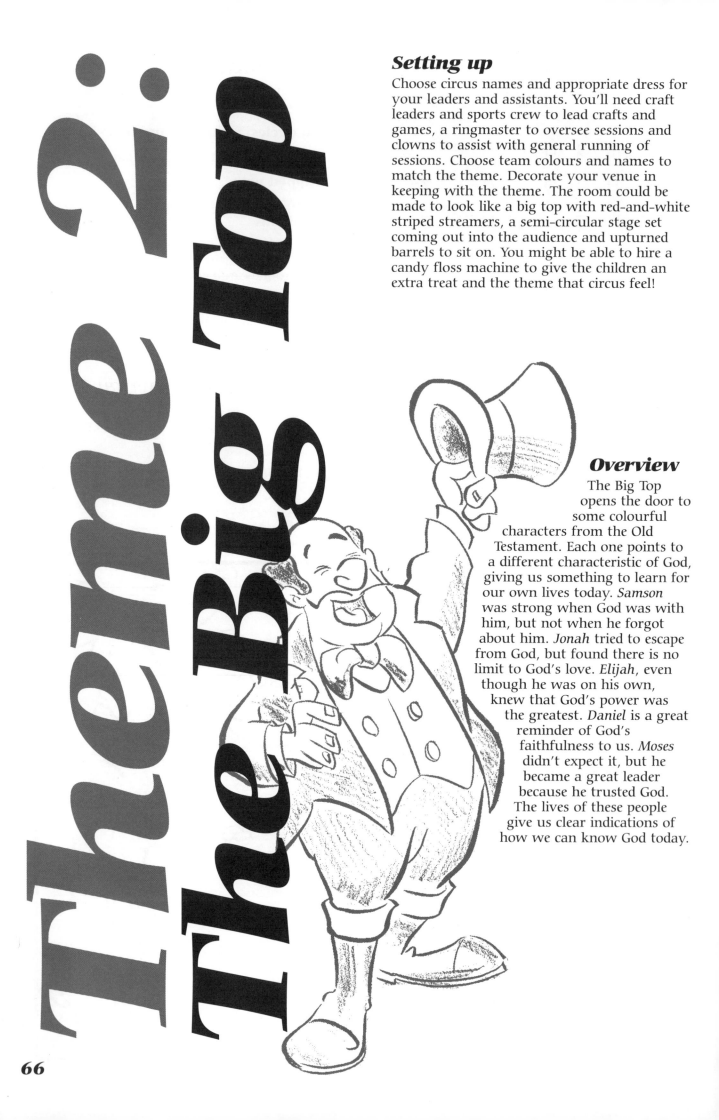

Theme 2: The Big Top

Setting up

Choose circus names and appropriate dress for your leaders and assistants. You'll need craft leaders and sports crew to lead crafts and games, a ringmaster to oversee sessions and clowns to assist with general running of sessions. Choose team colours and names to match the theme. Decorate your venue in keeping with the theme. The room could be made to look like a big top with red-and-white striped streamers, a semi-circular stage set coming out into the audience and upturned barrels to sit on. You might be able to hire a candy floss machine to give the children an extra treat and the theme that circus feel!

Overview

The Big Top opens the door to some colourful characters from the Old Testament. Each one points to a different characteristic of God, giving us something to learn for our own lives today. *Samson* was strong when God was with him, but not when he forgot about him. *Jonah* tried to escape from God, but found there is no limit to God's love. *Elijah*, even though he was on his own, knew that God's power was the greatest. *Daniel* is a great reminder of God's faithfulness to us. *Moses* didn't expect it, but he became a great leader because he trusted God. The lives of these people give us clear indications of how we can know God today.

Crafts

Finger puppet clowns

For each child you will need:

Scraps of coloured felt

Darning needle

Embroidery thread

Glue

1. Cut out clown body shapes, back and front, using template A.
2. Sew or glue body shapes together.
3. Cut out clown using template B, colour and stick to body shape.

Template A

Template B

Clown skittles

For each child you will need:

5 cardboard tubes

5 card circles, 8 cm in diameter

5 strips of paper, 10 cm x 15 cm

Felt tipped pens

For ball: 50 gm dried lentils, cling film, two balloons

1. Draw body of circus characters onto strips of paper and colour in with felt tipped pens. Glue around cardboard tubes.
2. Draw face on one side of card circle, back of head on reverse.
3. Cut two small slits on card circle, 2 cm in from outside edges.
4. Secure card circle to tube by slotting tube into slits.
5. To make ball: wrap lentils in cling film; cut neck off balloons; open out neck of first balloon and pull over lentils. Repeat with second balloon, pulling over first balloon so neck of first balloon is covered.

Clown masks

For each child you will need:

Template on next page, photocopied or traced onto paper

Strong card or paper plate

Shirring elastic

Colouring crayons or felt tipped pens

1. Cut out mask shapes and colour in.
2. Glue onto strong card of paper plate.
3. Make small holes in opposite sides of mask (place clear sticky tape where you intend to make the holes to prevent the card from tearing and use a hole punch to make the hole). Thread shirring elastic through holes to finish mask.

**Clown Mask
template**

Juggling balls

For each child you will need:

80 gm dried lentils

cling film

2 balloons

1. Using 20 gm lentils for each juggling ball, wrap lentils in cling film.
2. Cut narrow neck off balloons.
3. Open out neck of first balloon and pull over lentils. Repeat with second balloon, pulling over first balloon so neck of first balloon is covered.

Pop-up clowns

For each child you will need:

One cardboard tube

Strip of paper 10 cm x 15 cm

Strip of strong card 3.5 cm x 9 cm

Felt tipped pens

Drinking straw

Sticky tape

1. Draw Big Top stripes onto strip of paper and colour in.
2. Glue coloured in strip around cardboard tube, stripes side out.
3. Cut clown character out of strip of strong card.
4. Fix top of drinking straw to back of clown character.
5. Push straw up through the tube to make the clown 'pop up' out of Big Top.

Memory verse money boxes

For each child you will need:

One small, clean, empty cocoa or custard drum

Strip of paper to cover drum

Circle of card large enough to form into shallow cone shape on top of drum

Felt tipped pens

Glue

Plain sticky label

1. Draw Big Top stripes onto strip of paper and colour in.
2. Glue to drum.
3. Draw Big Top Stripes onto circle of card so that when cone shape is formed stripes match those around the drum.

3. Turn drum upside down so that lid is underneath.
4. Form circle of card into cone shape by slitting from edge to centre and gluing long sides together.
5. Fix cone to top of drum (unlidded end).
6. Cut horizontal slit in side of drum, 5 cm x 1 cm.
7. Write memory verse for day on sticky label and stick onto Big Top money box.

Cardboard strong men

For each child you will need:

Template on following page, photocopied or traced onto cartridge paper

Felt tipped pens

Four split pin fasteners

Modelling clay and darning needle

1. Cut out strong-man body and limbs, and colour in.
2. Make holes to affix limbs to body by placing modelling clay under card and making neat hole with darning needle
3. Fasten limbs to body with split pin fasteners.

Circus mobiles

For each child you will need:

Templates on following page 71 photocopied or traced onto cartridge paper

Felt tipped pens

Darning needle

Buttonhole thread

Thin, strong wire

1. Cut out card shapes and colour in.
2. Cut two lengths of wire, 30 cm each.
3. Form each end of wire into small loop.
4. Thread buttonhole thread through card shapes and tie off end.
5. Tie other end through wire loop (one shape on each loop).
6. Space wire lengths apart with buttonhole thread.
7. Make hanger for top of mobile with buttonhole thread.

Badges

See instructions on page 33 of Adventure Cruise theme.

Frieze

See instructions on page 33 of Adventure Cruise theme.

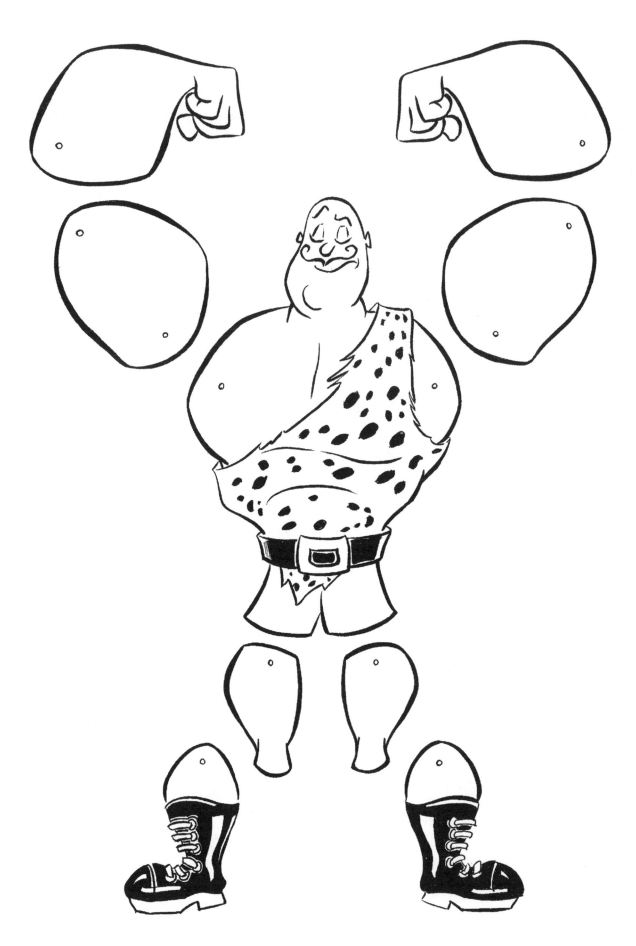

Template for Cardboard Strongman

**Circus
Mobile
Card
Shapes**

Games

The day the circus came to town

Split the children into teams of ten. Sit the children on the floor one behind the other in their teams. Give each child a character or an item to do with the circus. Tell them a story which includes all the different characters and items. Every time the child hears their character or item they have to run clockwise round their team and back to their place. The first one back gains a point for their team.

The characters and items are:

Child 1: Ringmaster

Child 2: Clowns

Child 3: Flying trapeze

Child 4: Elephants

Child 5: Tightrope walker

Child 6: Audience

Child 7: Big top

Child 8: Jugglers

Child 9: Strong man

Child 10: Candyfloss

If you don't have enough children to have ten in each team, miss the same characters/items off the list for each team.

Tell the following story SLOWLY!!

One summer day, lots of lorries started to arrive; the circus had come to town! The RINGMASTER (*children who are ringmasters run*) organized the performers and soon the BIG TOP started to go up. The STRONG MAN was asked to start knocking the pegs in. Then the RINGMASTER called the ELEPHANT riders and asked them to get the poles into position. Then the RINGMASTER told the FLYING TRAPEZE artists and the TIGHTROPE WALKERS to climb the poles and start to put the stripy red canvas onto the poles. 'CLOWNS!' he shouted, 'Get onto your stilts and attach the sides!' The BIG TOP soon started to take shape. The JUGGLERS were practising with flaming hoops and the CANDYFLOSS seller poured the sugar into his CANDYFLOSS machine. Everyone was busy. The RINGMASTER was giving his orders, the CLOWNS were clowning around, the ELEPHANTS were practising sitting on their tubs and waving their trunks in the air. 'I hope we get a good AUDIENCE tonight', said the FLYING TRAPEZE artist to the TIGHTROPE WALKER. The STRONG MAN walked a bit too close to the JUGGLERS. 'Here! Watch out where you're throwing those hoops, you nearly singed my whiskers'! he yelled. The CANDYFLOSS seller started up his CANDYFLOSS machine when he saw the AUDIENCE coming up the hill. 'The BIG TOP will be full tonight!' cried the RINGMASTER in delight. The ELEPHANTS waved their trunks in excitement. The RINGMASTER welcomed the AUDIENCE as they walked towards the BIG TOP. The CLOWNS showed the AUDIENCE to their seats, making the children laugh with their jokes and antics. The ELEPHANTS squirted water at everybody. The CANDYFLOSS seller was very busy. Soon it was time for the show to start. The RINGMASTER announced the different acts. First came the ELEPHANTS, parading around in their fine head-dresses and doing amazing balancing acts on their tubs. Then the FLYING TRAPEZE artists flew through the air, soaring and diving above the heads of the AUDIENCE, high up at the top of the BIG TOP. The AUDIENCE gasped in amazement. Then the STRONG MAN came into the ring, with the CANDYFLOSS seller sitting on his strong shoulders and they treated the children in the AUDIENCE to sticks of pink, sticky CANDYFLOSS. The JUGGLERS made the AUDIENCE gasp with their daring act. The BIG TOP was buzzing with excitement. The CLOWNS tried to follow the TIGHTROPE WALKER across the tightrope. The AUDIENCE roared with laughter. At last it was time for the grand finale. Out came the ELEPHANTS waving their trunks, the FLYING TRAPEZE artists leaping and doing somersaults, the TIGHTROPE WALKER balanced on his tightrope, the STRONG MAN bent down and lifted two small children from the AUDIENCE and carefully balanced them on his huge shoulders, the JUGGLERS walked in, juggling brightly coloured clubs. The RINGMASTER announced the end of the show and the CANDYFLOSS seller sold the last little scrap from his CANDYFLOSS machine. The AUDIENCE left and the BIG TOP was empty. 'What a great night!' said the AUDIENCE as they left for home. And EVERYONE agreed! (*Everyone gets up and runs round where their team would be and back to their place*) THE END!

Knock-down clowns

For this game you need to make a skittle out of two buckets. Place the first bucket the right way up and put the second bucket upside down on top of it. Stick on coloured shapes to make a face—two clown eyes, a clown nose and a clown mouth, a bow tie and a hat. You need two bean bags for each team.

Split the children into two equal teams. Sit them down at different sides of the room, facing each other. Number 1–15 down one side of the room and then come up the other side, numbering 1–15 (so that the number 1s are at opposite ends of the room). Put the clown skittle in the middle of the room, take two chairs and place one either side of the clown skittle, both about twelve paces from the skittle. Place a bean bag under each chair.

Give the two teams names—for example 'Jugglers' and 'Acrobats'. Each team will have the chair on its left.

When you call a number, both children with that number race to their chair, take the bean bag from under the chair, stand on the chair and with one throw try to knock down the clown. They only win a point if they are the first to knock down the clown. The clown and the bean bags are then re-instated and another number is called until everyone has had a go. The team with the most points is the winner. It is a good idea to have a leader hold each chair so that it won't tip.

Musical performers

The children choose a circus performance to practise. Suggestions could include:

Juggler: Pretend to juggle

Elephant and rider: Two team up, one rides on the other's back

Flying trapeze: Swing backwards and forwards with arms above head

Strong man: Pretend to hammer in the tent pegs

Tightrope walker: Pretend to balance on a tightrope

Ring master: Crack a pretend whip and wave a pretend top hat

Acrobat: Do somersaults

Lion tamer: Pretend to tame the lions

Seal: Pretend to balance ball on nose and clap hands

When the music plays the children practise their chosen performance. When the music stops they have to freeze their pose. The leaders then come round pretending to be the clowns and try to make the children laugh. Anyone who laughs or moves is out of the game. They then become the audience, sitting round the edge of the room and cheering on the players who are left in. Restart the music and continue the game until only one person is left.

Lions' tails

Cut a ball of string into enough pieces to provide each child with a 'tail'. Each tail needs to be about 50 cm long. The children tuck their tails loosely into the back of their clothing at waist level. Someone is chosen to be the lion tamer. The lion tamer chases the lions and tries to catch hold of their tails, pulling them away from the lion. (The tails mustn't be tied on.) The lion tamer keeps all the tails he catches. The winner is the last person left with a tail. That person becomes the lion tamer in the next game.

Performing seals

Split the children into equal teams, with ideally no more than ten in each team, and line the teams up each side of the room. You need an inflated balloon for each team. Give the person at the head of each team a balloon. When you shout 'go!' they have to pass the balloon down the line over their heads to the last person. The last competitors then crawl under the legs of their team, pushing the balloon as they go, to the front of the line. They then pass the balloon down the line, over people's heads, and so on until every team member has had a turn. The team who get back to the right order first are the winners.

Day 1

 GOD'S STRENGTH—*Strong man, Samson, disobeys God*

 Philippians 4:13 'I can do all things, through him who gives me strength.'

 Samson has a God-given gift, but he uses it unwisely. His story shows how he failed God, but God still answered his prayer. God gives gifts to each one of us, but he wants us to use them wisely.

Day 2

 GOD'S LOVE—*Escape artist, Jonah, runs away*

 Romans 8:38–39 'I am certain that. . . nothing can separate us from the love of God.'

 Jonah knew what God wanted him to do, but he failed to do it. In trying to escape from God, he ended up having to escape from a fish! At last Jonah did as God asked and took God's message to Nineveh. God's love saved the Ninevites and taught Jonah a lesson. When we know God is asking us to do something for him, we must trust that he knows what he is doing.

Day 3

 GOD'S POWER—*Fire-eater, Elijah, goes it alone for God*

 2 Corinthians 12:9 'My grace is sufficient for you, my power is made perfect in weakness.'

 Elijah had to face the taunts from the crowd, but he believed that God was there. Elijah was given the opportunity to show unbelievers that God's power is supreme. We must be ready to put our own faith into action, confident that God won't let us down.

Day 4

 GOD'S FAITHFULNESS—*Lion-tamer, Daniel, faces the savage beasts*

 2 Timothy 4:7 'I have done my best in the race, run the full distance and kept my faith.'

 Throughout his life Daniel was faithful to God. God stuck close to Daniel through thick and thin and showed him just how faithful a God he was. God will never leave us, no matter what our situation.

Day 5

 GOD'S LEADERSHIP— *Ringmaster, Moses, knows who's really in charge*

 Matthew 28:20 'I will be with you always, to the end of the age.'

 When God asked Moses to lead the Israelites to the promised land, Moses didn't think he was up to it, but he soon found out that with God's help anything is possible.

Day 1

GOD'S STRENGTH

Strong man, Samson, disobeys God

Aim

To show the contrast between our strength and God's strength and to show how trying to cope on our own ultimately loses meaning if God is not involved.

Warm up

This energy blast involves as much as your imagination can cope with. All you need is some suitable backing music and you're off! Start with some gentle muscle-man poses! Try to make them as amusing as possible. Why not try some of these:

1) Both arms flexing muscles

2)'Bruce Forsyth' style fist on forehead

3) Arms clenched inwards, puffing up chest

4) Fingers locked in front of chest

5) Flex knees, hands on hips and swivel at waist etc.

End with some simple 'strong-man' training exercises such as:

● *Weight-lifting: Start off crouched down, straining hard as you lift imaginary weights off the ground, pausing at chest height with a big final push stretching your arms above your head. Then back down again; but remember— it's heavy!*

● *Press-ups: Find a space where you won't kick any one in the head! Then from a lying position push up on your arms— straight backs, please! Remember to add plenty of good grunts and groans to build the tension!*

● *On the spot jogging: Do some on-the-spot jogging. Slowly at first, then speeding up. Try the high-knees variety as well, lifting your knees as high as you can as you jog along—going nowhere very fast!*

Theme Song

The theme song is 'Roll on up to the Big Top'. The sheet music can be found in Appendix B on page 146. The song can be found on the *Ultimate Holiday Club* audio cassette, available from your local Christian bookshop, or, in case of difficulty, direct from BRF.

Theme illustration

With God's strength we can do things that we certainly couldn't do without his help. You will need a couple of volunteers—a small girl and a bigger lad who understand that they are to mime an arm-wrestling contest. The odds being heavily and obviously stacked in the boy's favour, the girl should pretend to lose dismally in the first round (*Encourage audience participation cheering the contestants on, etc.*). Then arrange for your biggest and beefiest leader to appear on the scene, take up position behind the girl, with her hand in his so they take on the lad together. (*More audience participation*). Bring out the point that it's like that with God. With his help we can do everything.

Drama/Adventure story

The Watt family's circus adventure: I

This is a four-part contemporary story which picks up the teaching for the week, revealing it in daily installments. The story outline can be adapted to be performed as a drama, a dramatized narration, or read as a story. Feel free to embellish and adapt the outline to suit your own situation. A hand-puppet dog could be used for Whatnot. Play the Watt Family theme tune as the cast come on stage and again at the end of the drama (see Appendix B, page 146, also on cassette, see page 160).

The summer holidays have begun at last and Rick and Wendy Watt are looking forward to the long break. They have just woken from a long lie-in on day one, and are settling down to a breakfast of Whatabix (three each) and a good

video, when their little dog Whatnot starts barking fiercely—a sure sign that the postman is coming up the drive.

'What a row, Whatnot, do give it a miss!' they yell at him. There's a letter lying on the mat addressed to the kids—Rick and Wendy Watt, Watt Street, Wattford, Wattshire. What writing! What huge spidery scrawl creeping across the front of the envelope!

The kids tear open the letter and who should it be from but Great Uncle Waldo! Now, Great Uncle Waldo is the kids' favourite uncle. He's full of good humour, full of bright ideas and, best of all, the ringmaster of his very own circus: The Watt Brothers' Circus. To their delight the kids discover, when they've sorted out Great Uncle Waldo's spidery scrawl, that the Watt Brother's Circus is coming to town! Hooray! What a wonderful invitation! A whole

week helping out at the circus. What fun! What a great start to the holidays!

Suddenly the kids realize that the date Great Uncle Waldo has given for the circus' arrival is today's date. What short notice! They down their Whatabix, switch off the video (what good kids) and call out 'Walkies, Whatnot!' Then they set off for the field where the circus is to be held.

But what's this? When they arrive, the Big Top is there, the caravans are there, the candyfloss machine is there, but there's no one around. What? No one around? Where's everyone gone? What's happened to them. The kids go into the Big Top and there, sitting on an upturned barrel in the middle of the ring, is Great Uncle Waldo with the strong-man at his side. Great Uncle Waldo doesn't look happy. In fact Great Uncle Waldo looks somewhat *un*happy, and somewhat confused. He hardly takes any notice at all of Whatnot's friendly and rather wet greeting. 'Whatever's the matter, Great Uncle Waldo?' cry the Watt kids. Great Uncle Waldo looks up at them as they run over to him and holds out a crumpled letter which he's been clutching in his hand.

What's this? It's written in large, badly formed letters. It says 'I HAVE KIDNAPPED YOUR PERFORMERS. HA HA!' and it's signed 'The hooded man'. What a to-do!

'It's a sell-out tonight, I've got a full house for tonight's show and no performers!' wails Great Uncle Waldo. 'I can't put on a show by myself! What am I going to do?' What indeed! The strong-man will do what he can—but he can't do everything! Rick and Wendy get their thinking caps on and try to come up with a plan to help Great Uncle Waldo—after all he is their favourite uncle. What can they do? Can you give them any ideas, everybody? (*Audience responds*)

The Watt kids think of the things they are good at. They soon discover that each is only good at one thing—Wendy can only pull funny faces and Rick can only tell silly jokes. In a circus you have to be able to put all your strengths together—that's what makes the circus such good fun! Great Uncle Waldo tries hard to encourage them, but it's no good, they'd need to have tons of practice before they could be even a tiny bit as good as the circus performers.

Great Uncle Waldo and the Watt kids are so busy trying to sort something out they don't notice that the hooded man has crept into the back of the audience and is making his way stealthily towards the stage. (*Audience responds*) It's no good; however much the audience try to warn them, they don't see the hooded man. He creeps up behind the strong-man and, quick as a flash ties him up and kidnaps him too! What a to-do! Where's he gone? Now they won't even be able to rely on the strong-man's support. WHAT ARE THEY GOING TO DO?? YOU'LL HAVE TO WAIT UNTIL TOMORROW TO FIND OUT WHAT HAPPENS NEXT. . .

Drama/Adventure story link

Great Uncle Waldo and the Watt family were not having a very good day. Everything seemed to be going wrong. Do you every have days like that when nothing goes right? Sometimes it's hard to keep going when we keep getting knocked back. Life as a Christian is not always easy. It's very hard going, but God can help us and give us the strength to do the right thing sometimes.
The Watt kids realized that each of them was good at one thing. God has given us each of us special gifts, although possibly not those of a circus performer! God loves us to use our special gifts for him—doing the things we are good at to help other people.

Memory verse

Philippians 4:13 'I can do all things through him who gives me strength'. This verse flows with a natural rhythm and lends itself to a number of formats, such as:

A rap: Philippians//Chapter Four//Verse Thirteen//I can do//all things//through him//who gives me strength///
    Underlined type = the syllable accentuated by the beat. / = clap or similar at the end of each bar.

An echo: As above, but with the words echoed where the claps would be.

A song: The sheet music for this can be found in Appendix B on page 146. The song can be found on the *Ultimate Holiday Club Guide* cassette, available from your local Christian bookshop, or, in case of difficulty, direct from BRF.

Quiz

Questions could include:

Where in the Bible will you find today's memory verse?
    Philippians 4:13

What is the name of the family in the drama?
    Yes, that's right!

Who is in charge of the circus?
    Great Uncle Waldo

What have we saved for you (according to the theme song?)
    A ringside seat

The principles of using clowns are outlined in Part One on page 16. Here is their first entrance. Clown One introduces himself and his skills. Then Clown Two arrives and shows that two are better than one. Use the outline below to ad-lib your own script. Decide on names for your clowns.

Day 1: Super clowns!

A leader sets the scene by explaining that God gives each of us gifts. The gifts he gives us are special. God's gifts help us to learn more about him and to stand up for what is right. God's gifts also help us to tell other people about him and help us to know when other people need our help. God gives his gifts to everyone who believes in him, but he wants us to use his gifts wisely. The leader says he knows someone who's got a gift for making us laugh. I wonder if he's around? Let's give him a call. The leader encourages audience to call out for Clown A.

Clown A comes on to the stage and does a few tricks for the audience. Then he calls for Clown B. But Clown B doesn't want to come out. He's decided that he doesn't want to be a clown anymore because everyone laughs at him all the time. He looks very unhappy. Suddenly he has a bright idea. He'll be a strong-man. Everyone admires the strong-man and no one would dare to laugh at *him*! Clown B does some strong-man poses. Clown A stands by watching and then starts to laugh. Clown B wants to know what's so funny. Clown A explains that to be a strong-man you have to be strong! He tests Clown B's muscles—nothing there! Clown B looks even unhappier. He goes off the stage. Clown A carries on doing tricks while Clown B is gone.

Clown B reappears. He's carrying some toy weights. He makes out that they are really heavy. He does a weight-lifting act with them to prove how strong he is. Clown A pretends to look impressed. Wow! Look at those muscles! Clown B makes a big show of lifting the weights above his head. Clown A gets the audience to clap and cheer. He gives the audience a big wink as if to say, 'we are impressed, aren't we!' Clown B carries on showing off, lifting the weights with one hand, on one foot etc. while Clown A continues to get the audience to respond. All this applause goes to Clown B's head. He starts to strut around the stage, showing off to the audience and obviously full of his own importance.

Clown A decides Clown B is in danger of getting rather a swollen head! He picks a very small child from the audience and invites them on to the stage. He says to the child, 'You'd better take that off him before he hurts himself. His head is getting too big for his boots!' He taps Clown B on the shoulder and beckons the child to take the weights.

The child picks them up easily. Clown B looks amazed and then he is annoyed. Clown A has made everyone laugh at him again! Clown B sits down with his head in his hands. He says that he's sick of being a clown and having everyone laugh at him. Clown A has given the game away and spoilt his chance to be somebody special.

But finally, Clown A tells him that he *is* somebody special—he's a great clown. He makes people happy. Clown B looks up. Does he? How does he make people happy? Clown A explains to Clown B that he's so good at what he does that everybody loves him because he makes them laugh. Clown B is amazed. He gets up and asks the audience if this is true. (*Audience responds*) Together the two clowns practise some clowning. Clown A picks up the weights. Cor—they really are heavy, aren't they! They go off stage together. Bye-bye everyone!

Puppets

Bert: Come on Lucy! Where are you?

Lucy: I'm coming! I'm just coming! (*She appears—out of breath*)

Bert: Where have you been?

Lucy: I've been helping Mum and Dad.

Bert: That's very good of you, Lucy. Are you feeling OK?

Lucy: (*Slightly put out*) Yes, I am, thank you very much. I help Mum and Dad quite often.

Bert: Well, what were you doing to help?

Lucy: I got up really early and unpacked and put away all the shopping.

Bert: Wow! All by yourself?

Lucy: Yes, all by myself!

Bert: That was very kind of you. How did you get on?

Lucy: Well, let me see. . . I unpacked carrots and fish fingers and chocolate and yoghurts and milk and bananas. . .

Bert: You always were a bit of a banana!

Lucy: Be-e-e-r-r-t-t-t!!

Bert: Sorry! What else?

Lucy: And tea bags and ice cream and chocolate and cornflakes and mars bars and apples and chocolate and cheese and tomatoes and, and, and. . .

Bert: Wow! How on earth did you find the space for it all?

Lucy: Well, I ate the chocolate. And then I ran in to a little bit of a problem.

Bert: What do you mean?

Lucy: Well, because there were so many things everywhere I only unpacked them onto the kitchen floor.

Bert: Well, what did you do with them then?

Lucy: Well, I couldn't put any more away so I left and hurried off here.

Bert: You left things all over the kitchen floor?

Lucy: Yes, you see I really couldn't do any more, and I didn't want to be late meeting you. . .

Bert: You can't leave it there, Lucy—the ice cream will melt and somebody might trip over it all.

Lucy: I know, but I couldn't carry on any more.

Bert: Why don't I give you a hand—two

people are better than one.

Lucy: Would you, really?

Bert: Of course I will, Lucy. That's what friends are for!

Lucy: Oh, thank you Bert. Come on then, let's go!

Bert: Say 'goodbye', Lucy.

Lucy: Goodbye, Lucy!

Bert: Goodbye, everyone.

Bible story

This is the story of Samson, who was only strong when God was with him. Judges, chapters 13–16.

Key points

- *Samson's strength was a special gift from God to use for God's people, the Israelites.*
- *God wanted to use Samson as a key figure for the good of his people.*
- *The secret of Samson's strength was symbolized by his long hair and God had warned him never to have it cut off.*
- *Samson disobeyed God by not listening to the way God wanted him to live.*
- *Samson used his strength to go his own way.*
- *Samson lost his strength when God left him.*
- *Samson finally realized that he had let God down.*
- *God didn't let Samson down when he prayed to him.*

Style suggestion

Cast: Narrator and two others (A and B)

Narr: *God chooses to use ordinary people; people like you and me. He doesn't use super-brave super-heroes!*

A: *Why?*

Narr: *Why what?*

A: *Why doesn't God use super-brave super-heroes? People like the Gladiators, or He Man or Superman. Why doesn't God make us strong like them, then no one would dare argue with us, and we could make sure that everyone treated each other fairly! It would be great!*

B: *Yeah! Excellent idea! I'd have big muscles like. . . (name of current muscle-man hero—B flexes his muscles.)*

Narr: *It wouldn't work!*

A and B: *How do you know?!?*

Narr: *Because God did use a sort of super-hero once—he was at least 1,000 times stronger than anyone else!*

A and B: *Wow!*

Narr: *(Shouts) GIVE ME AN 'S'!*

A and B: *(Encourage audience to join in and all shout) 'S'*

Narr: *GIVE ME AN 'A' (echo 'A')*

Narr: *GIVE ME AN 'M' (echo 'M')*

Narr: *GIVE ME AN 'S' (echo 'S')*

Narr: *GIVE ME AN 'O' (echo 'O')*

Narr: *GIVE ME AN 'N' (echo 'N')*

Narr: *Who have you got? S-A-M-S-O-N!*

A: *He was STRONG!*

B: *He was BRAVE!*

A: *He was BIG!*

B: *He was. . .*

Narr: *(Interrupts) Hang on a minute, he was strong because God had made him strong! And he was brave, but the Bible doesn't say that he was big! In fact, I don't think he can have been, because his enemies didn't understand why he was so strong. I reckon he was quite normal looking—but he was incredibly strong!*

A: *Why was he so strong?*

Narr: *Well, when he was born God decided to give him a special gift. He made him a Nazirite—which means that he had to be brought up in a special way. He couldn't drink wine or beer, or eat certain foods and—wait for it—he couldn't ever, ever have a hair cut!*

A and B: *What never! Never, never, never, never, never. . .*

Narr: *No! Never! God set him apart to rescue the people of Israel from their enemies, the Philistines.*

A: *So Samson was born!*

B: *(Shouts) GIVE ME AN 'S'!*

A: *(Encourage audience to join in and all shout) 'S'*

B: *GIVE ME AN 'A' (echo 'A')*

A: *GIVE ME AN 'M' (echo 'M')*

B: *GIVE ME AN 'S' (echo 'S')*

A: *GIVE ME AN 'O' (echo 'O')*

B: *GIVE ME AN 'N' (echo 'N')*

A: *Who have you got? S-A-M-S-O-N!*

B: *He was STRONG!*

A: *He was BRAVE!*

B: *He was BIG!*

A: *He was. . .*

Narr: *. . . he was born. And God blessed him and he grew very strong.*

A: *Go, Samson! Go, go, go!*

Narr: *One day Samson was on his way to the Philistine camp when a lion attacked him.*

B: *Oh no! Our hero! Run, Samson! Run, run, run!*

Narr: *Don't be daft! The lion didn't stand a chance!*

A: *You've picked on the wrong guy this time!*

Narr: *He certainly had! Samson tore the lion to pieces. . . and continued on his way to the Philistine camp.*

B: He was on his way to kill them all!

Narr: No! Not this time! He had fallen in love with a Philistine girl.

A: What! Fallen in love with the enemy!

Narr: Well, yes. That was Samson's biggest mistake, he always fell in love with the wrong girl.

A: Did he get on with her family?

Narr: No way! Samson had lots of battles against the Philistines.

B: Go, Samson! Go, go, go!

A: Will they beat him? No, no, no!

A and B: (Chant above twice).

Narr: That's right. Samson lead the Israelites for twenty years. But he started to forget about God.

A: I bet he was a great warrior!

Narr: Well, yes. But he fell in love with yet another Philistine girl, and the Philistines saw their chance. They promised to make her rich if she found out the secret of Samson's strength.

B: So she nagged him. . .

A: And she chivvied him. . .

B: And she henpecked him. . .

B: And she pestered him. . .

Narr: Until he eventually told her his secret.

A: About how he was a Nazirite.

B: And set apart by God.

A: And how his hair must never be cut.

B: Because that was the sign of his special strength.

Narr: So Delilah, that was her name, lulled Samson to sleep in her lap. And then one of the Philistines came and paid her the money they'd promised her.

A: And cut off his hair.

B: Snip, snip, snip!

A: Oh my!

Narr: Then she shouted. . .

B: Samson! The Philistines are coming!

Narr: And he woke up ready to fight. But his strength had gone, God had left him and Delilah laughed at him.

A: What a meany!

B: What a disgrace!

Narr: So the Philistines took him away as their prisoner, blinded him and chained him up.

A: Down with the baddies!

B: Booo!

Narr: They made Samson grind the mill in the prison. But something was happening. . .

A: His hair began to grow!

B: He had forgotten God.

A: But, God hadn't forgotten him!

B: Go, Samson! Go, go, go!

Narr: The Philistines had a celebration and they brought Samson into their great hall to entertain them. Samson said to the boy who was leading him. . .

A: Let me touch the pillars that hold up the building. I want to lean on them.

Narr: And Samson prayed to God. . .

B: Please, God, give me my strength back just once more.

Narr: And Samson took hold of the pillars and pushed with all his might.

A: He was amazingly strong!

Narr: No, he was still weak. But God is strong.

B: The building fell down on the five Philistine kings and everyone else.

A: Including Samson.

Narr: Samson killed more people at his death than he had killed during his life.

A: And so God never used a super-hero again?

Narr: No, he prefers to use people like us.

B: Weak.

A: Ordinary.

A and B: Like you and me.

Narr: But we can trust God and he is strong!

All: And he gives us the strength to do what he wants us to do!

The Samson rap

There's a story in the Bible of a strong, strong man.

Samson is his name, from a place called Dan.

Now Samson's strength was special, 'cos God gave it him.

He had to fight the Philistines, and God said he would win!

Yes Samson's strength was special, it wasn't here, (flex arms) or there. (puff out chest)

Samson's strength was a gift from God—the sign was his long hair!

Now, folks, if God asks for your help, you have to get it right.

It's no good on your own, 'cos you're bound to lose the fight.

Stick close to what you know God wants and listen to his voice

He'll stay with you and help you win—and then you will rejoice.

Remember how the sign of strength was Samson's uncut hair?

Well, Samson forgot he was a man of God and didn't take much care!

He fought with lions, he played some tricks and threw his weight around.

He fell in love with a Philistine girl and she brought him to the ground.

Yes, Delilah was a Philistine, she wasn't on God's side;

She squeezed Sam's secret out of him when she became his bride.

As soon as she knew why Sam was strong, she saw her path was clear!

She called her friends while Samson slept and they cut off all his hair.

And where was Sam when he awoke? O boy, he was in a plight!

He'd been tied up and couldn't move, though he tried with all his might!

The cruel Philistines took him off to jail, a weak and broken man

They blinded him and chained him up, they fixed our man from Dan.

Now what happens when your hair is cut? It grows again—that's right!

Well, Samson remembered he was a man of God, and he prayed with all his might.

He said he was sorry he'd forgotten God—the God who gave him strength.

And, naturally, his hair began to grow—and it grew to quite a length.

The Philistines didn't realize what was happening, which was odd.

(I suppose they had forgotten that Sam's strength was a gift from God.)

They dragged Sam into a great big hall to celebrate their win,

And laughed aloud at the thought of how they'd taken Samson in.

But Samson took the pillars of the hall between his great big hands,

And pulled and pushed while he prayed to God—and they crumbled—just like sand.

Ol' Samson brought the house down, on the Philistines and all,

'Cos at last he'd seen just who was boss, and he listened to God's call.

So that's the story of Samson, folks, and although I spoke at length,

Just you remember you can do anything through him WHO GIVES YOU STRENGTH!

Quiz 2, memory verse recap, prayer and theme song

The Big Top

GOD'S STRENGTH—*Strongman Samson*

Lead Samson to the temple

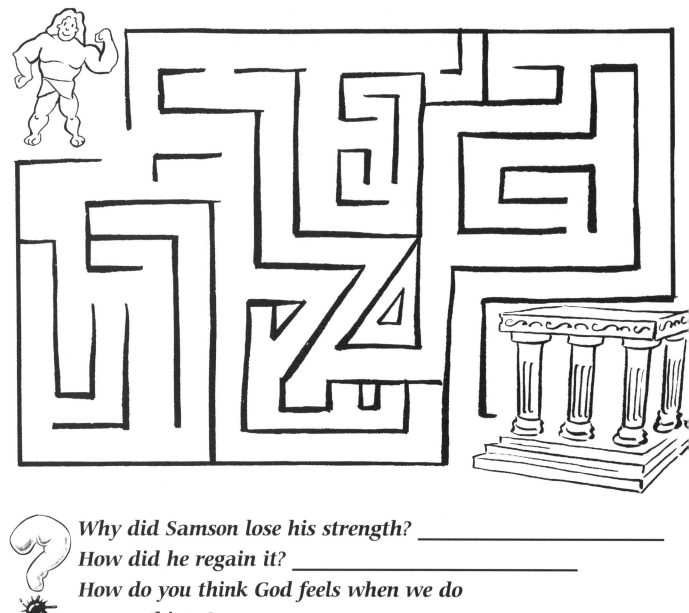

Why did Samson lose his strength? _____

How did he regain it? _____

How do you think God feels when we do
wrong things? _____

Samson finally used his strength to do what God wanted. How can we
do what God wants, using the abilities he has given us?

_____

Write your answers on the lines, or draw a picture in the space below.

Where does today's memory verse come from?

Chapter 4 verse 13

 Fill in the missing letters to complete the memory verse.

I c__ _o e___y_____ __r___h _i_ w__ __v__ _e _t___g__

Colour in the picture of Strongman Samson

Delilah's Delightfully Difficult Wordsearch

```
t x e t i r i z a n
e h j a w b o n e t
m y a s b i h p a s
p h i l i s t i n e
l i i d i n g u o p
e n l e b l n r s o
d s y l s o e n m r
y e d o a y r d a l
s h a v e r t r s f
s g n i r t s w o b
```

blind bowstrings delilah eyes
final jawbone loom nazirite
philistine pillars ropes samson
shave strength temple

Which two words are missing on the wordsearch grid?

Day 2

GOD'S LOVE

Escape artist, Jonah, runs away

Aim

To show that we can try to run away from things that we don't want to face up to but, whatever we do, nothing can separate us from God and his love for us.

Warm up

See Day 1

Theme song

See Day 1

Theme illustration

This illustration involves a reasonable level of interaction with the children. Ask them first to name the longest river or road they can think of (e.g. M1, Amazon). Then ask them to name the widest water or land mass (e.g. Atlantic Ocean, Sahara Desert). Then the highest building or mountain (e.g. Everest, Eiffel Tower). Finally, ask them to name the deepest ocean or lake (e.g. Loch Ness). Go on to explain that as big as those things are, they don't compare with God's love for us. The Bible explains that God's love for us is so vast that it is beyond comparison, and what's more there is nothing that can separate us from it.

Drama/Adventure story

The Watt family circus adventure: II

What did Rick and Wendy have for breakfast? What is the name of their dog? What did the letter from Great Uncle Waldo say? What was the matter with Great Uncle Waldo? What kind of faces can Wendy pull? What is the punchline to Rick's worst joke? What has the hooded man done with the strong-man?

Great Uncle Waldo realizes that the strong man has been kidnapped too. He can't believe it! What is he going to do? What indeed! He sits down on the upturned barrel with his head in his hands. He's ready to give up. The Watt kids don't know what to do either. They've completely run out of bright ideas. They half-heartedly try a few juggling and balancing tricks, but nothing seems to work.

Then who should walk into the big top but Grandma Watt. (*Comes in at back through audience*) Wendy and Rick are delighted to see her. They love their Grandma Watt very much, and she always seems to know what to do. They quickly tell her what has happened. Grandma Watt says, 'Hmm, let's have a think shall we?' She perches herself down on the edge of the circus' cannon and scratches her head thoughtfully, her knitting tucked under her arm. The Watt kids watch her, then they suddenly realize what she's sitting on and they have a bright idea at last!

'We know, Grandma Watt!' they say. 'Why don't we advertise a new act as the star attraction for tonight's bill? Let's say that there's going to be a spectacular flying cannon-ball act. We might be able to lure the hooded man into the big top—he's bound to be curious about how we're going to put on a show without our performers. Then we can capture him and make him tell us what he's done with our circus people.'

But Grandma Watt is not impressed. She shakes her head worriedly. 'And who's going to be the one going into the cannon?' She asks, wagging her knitting needles at them. Grandma Watt has a good point. The kids look at each other. What us? No way! Then they look at Great Uncle Waldo. What me? No way! Then they look at the audience. What them? No way! Is anybody prepared to do it? It's a big risk.

Then they look at Grandma Watt and suddenly a great slogan for a new act flashes into their minds. Of one mind and with one voice they say, 'THE HUMAN GRANNONBALL!' Yes! This is the lure they need to hoodwink the hooded man and save the day for Great Uncle Waldo!

'Grandma Watt, will you do it for us?' they ask. 'We need to be around to help Great Uncle Waldo capture the hooded man'. Grandma Watt is even less impressed. She definitely feels unloved. She doesn't want anything to do with the horrid hooded man and his horrid plans, and she certainly doesn't want to be catapulted out of a cannon because of him.

'It's too big a risk' she says. 'But, Grandma,' the kids respond, 'You know we love you, and wouldn't do anything to hurt you.' Great Uncle Waldo adds, 'Yes, that's right. but desperate times call for desperate measures. We all love the circus and to get the others back is going to involve some sort of risk.'

Great Uncle Waldo and the Watt kids think it's the perfect solution. They get their heads together to work out the details of their plan. Grandma doesn't want anything to do with it, she goes off stage in a huff. Just at that moment, while the Watt kids and Great Uncle Waldo are busy putting their plans together, the hooded man appears at the back of the stage and creeps slowly forward. (*Audience responds*) But by the time the audience has managed to attract Great Uncle Waldo and the kids' attention the hooded man has slipped away again. They carry on with their planning and eventually, coming to a decision, turn round to find Grandma gone. They search for her and ask for the audience's help to shout out for her (*Audience responds*). Finally, Grandma comes back on stage. They are sorry they hurt her feelings and explain that they don't really want her to go in the cannon. They just want her to pretend so they can advertise their new, amazing act—The Human Grannonball— thereby luring the hooded man into the open. Grandma starts to catch on to the idea. She really gets quite excited about it, peering bravely into the mouth of the cannon and practising her bows. Great Uncle Waldo and the kids go off to get some card and paint to make a poster for the new act.

The minute their backs are turned the hooded man re-appears on the stage. He creeps up behind Grandma Watt, who is quite oblivious to his presence, ties her up with a rope and kidnaps her too! Great Uncle Waldo and the kids come back on stage with the card and paints. They call out for Grandma and, when they get no reply, think she's gone off in a huff again. They ask for the audience to help call out for her. Slowly they realize that the audience is telling them that she's been captured. Oh no! They've let her down by not keeping an eye on her! What are they going to do now? They've lost the star of their new, amazing act. YOU'LL HAVE TO WAIT UNTIL TOMORROW TO FIND OUT WHAT HAPPENS NEXT. . .

Drama/Adventure story link

In order to help Great Uncle Waldo, Rick and Wendy knew they had to do something. After all, they loved their Great Uncle Waldo and his circus very much. When we love someone very much we are prepared to do anything to help each them. Jesus loves us so much that he was prepared to die on the cross so that we can be friends with God for ever. That's a very special love.

Memory verse

Ephesians 3:18 and Romans 8:38–39. 'How broad, how long, how high, how deep is the love of Christ. . . I am certain that nothing can separate us from his love.'

A song: The sheet music can be found in Appendix B on page 146. The song can be found on the *Ultimate Holiday Club Guide* cassette, available from your local Christian bookshop or, in case of difficulty, direct from BRF.

Quiz

Questions could include:
What did Grandma Watt sit on?
   A cannon
Who were the enemy in yesterday's story?
   The Philistines
Who did Samson fall in love with?
   Delilah
Who can give us strength?
   God

Day 2: The big 'let down'

A leader sets the scene by saying that we can all feel let down sometimes. Sometimes our friends let us down and sometimes our family lets us down. And sometimes we let other people down. But God won't let us down if we trust him. He always has our best interests at heart. The leader then says he knows someone who tries his best, but doesn't always get it right. I wonder if he's around? Let's given him a call. The leader encourages the audience to call out for Clown B.

Clown B comes on to the stage with a broom over his shoulder. He explains to the audience that Clown A has asked him to tidy up so that they can impress the ringmaster. He starts to sweep the floor, humming to himself as he goes. There are some buckets placed around the stage, some on the floor and some on tables. (Fill the buckets with either water, polystyrene bits or confetti-style coloured paper.) While he is sweeping clown B knocks a bucket off a table with the back of the broom handle. He doesn't notice. Then he accidentally puts his foot into one of the buckets. He doesn't try to take it off and the contents of the bucket spills over the floor as he goes.

Soon, Clown B is finding the sweeping up hard work. He, stops to take a rest. He tips the contents out of one of the buckets and upturns it. He sits down on it and pulls a banana out of his pocket, eats it and throws the skin over his shoulder. Then he gets up and carries on with his sweeping, wandering off stage as he goes.

Clown A walks on to the stage and is horrified by the mess. What has Clown B been doing?! Wait till I get my hands on him! He asks the audience if they have seen Clown B. (*Audience responds*) Clown A goes to find Clown B and they re-enter, Clown B being chased by Clown A. Clown A tells Clown B off for making such a mess. How could he be so stupid? They'll both get into trouble for this! Clown A stomps off stage, very angry. Clown B looks very sad. He too leaves the stage and then comes back on carrying a suitcase. He tells the audience that he's packed his bags and he's leaving. It's quite obvious that Clown A doesn't want him around any more. He thinks that Clown A doesn't love him because he's so useless. There's nothing for it but to leave the circus. He wanders sadly off the stage.

Clown A enters carrying a mop and broom. He's not looking angry now. He calls out to Clown B to come and help him clear up the mess. They'll soon get it done if they work together he says. He calls and calls. When there's no answer, he asks the audience if they know where Clown B is. (*Audience responds*) Clown A is horrified. 'He's gone? Where has he gone? He's left! But I need him, he's my partner clown. I know we both let each other down sometimes, but that doesn't mean we stop loving each other!' Clown A gets the audience to help him call for Clown B. They will have to shout very loud if they want him to hear them. (*Audience responds*)

Eventually Clown B comes back on to the stage, his suitcase still in his hand. 'What do you want?' he asks in a stern voice. Clown A explains how much he needs him. He says he's sorry that he got cross. Everybody loves Clown B, they don't want him to go, do they? (*Audience responds*) 'What, even after all the mess I've made?' says Clown B. Clown A assures him that everybody makes mistakes and together they clear up the mess, using the time to tease the audience with what's in the buckets etc. Finally they go off stage together. Bye-bye everyone!

Bert: (*calling*) Lucy. . . LUCY!
Lucy: What?
Bert: Come on, I've been waiting for you!
Lucy: Sorry. . . Hey! It's a lovely day!

Bert: Yes, it is.
Lucy: And this is a lovely place!
Bert: Not bad.
Lucy: And look at all those lovely people!
Bert: Most of them.
Lucy: And that's a lovely jumper your wearing, Bert!
Bert: Lucy, what on earth are you getting at?
Lucy: Well, I thought we were supposed to be talking about love today!
Bert: We are—but not that sort. . .
Lucy: Oh, what you mean. . . like. . . I love Ryan Giggs!
Bert: No, silly! A more special kind of love.
Lucy: Oh! I know. . . I love chocolate!
Bert: No, Lucy! Honestly, you are silly sometimes!
Lucy: Well, what then?
Bert: We're talking about God's love, which is greater than any other kind of love.
Lucy: What, more than chocolate?
Bert: Yes, Lucy. More than chocolate.
Lucy: Oh! Well, I'm sure if you explain it a bit more, Bert, I'll understand.
Bert: Well, why don't you sit back down and listen to this story. . .
Lucy: OK, Bert. Anything you say! Bye, bye everyone!
Bert: Bye, bye.

Bible story

Jonah tries to escape from God. Read the account in the book of Jonah, chapters 1–4.

Key points

- *Jonah was one of God's prophets, but God gave him a job which he didn't want to do. The Assyrians were Israel's deadly enemies and he didn't want God to save them.*
- *Jonah set out in the opposite direction. He was trying to escape from God—but he soon realized that he couldn't.*
- *In setting Jonah on the right course, God made such an impact that even the sailors promised to serve him.*
- *God gave Jonah time to straighten out his thoughts and he eventually did as God asked.*
- *God didn't give up on Jonah.*
- *God didn't even give up on the evil Ninevites and did everything he could to save them.*

Style suggestion

Cast: Narrator and two others (A and B)
Narr: Have you ever been asked to do something that you don't want to do?
A: So maybe you hide from the person who

asked you to do it!

B: Or just try to avoid them!

Narr: There was a man in the Bible who God spoke to.

A: Excellent! What a privilege to have God speak to you personally!

Narr: This man probably thought so at first. God said to him. . .

B: Jonah, you know the people of Nineveh? They are so wicked I've decided to destroy them.

Narr: Now you would have thought that Jonah would have said. . .

A: No, don't do that, Lord! Give them another chance!

Narr: But he didn't. He probably thought. . .

A: Good! Wipe them out, Lord! They deserve all they get—they're so wicked!

Narr: But God went on to say. . .

B: But if they say 'sorry' to me and turn from their wicked ways, I will forgive them.

Narr: And I can imagine Jonah thinking to himself. . .

A: No, no, no! You don't want to do that! (I'd hate to be the person God chooses to tell them to repent!)

B: So I'm sending you, Jonah!

A: What! No way, Lord! I'm not telling them! I'm off!

Narr: And off went Jonah. He went down to the port of Joppa and got on a ship that was going to Spain—the opposite direction to Nineveh!

B: What a ninny, fancy trying to escape from God!

Narr: Jonah hid himself below deck and went to sleep. Meanwhile. . . the wind began to blow. . .

A and B: (*Mime wind blowing*)

Narr: The waves became choppy. . .

A and B: (*Mime being tossed about*)

Narr: The sailors began to feel afraid. . .

A and B: (*Scream*)

Narr: Very afraid. . .

A and B: (*Scream louder*)

Narr: The waves became higher and higher. . .

A and B: (*Mime being thrown around the deck*)

Narr: And the sailors called out to their gods for help. . .

A and B: H E L P !

Narr: But nothing happened. . .

A and B: (*Look at each other helplessly*)

Narr: Then they had an idea. . .

A: Let's throw the cargo overboard to lighten the load!

B: Where's that bloke we took on board at Joppa?

Narr: So the captain went to look for Jonah, and there he was fast asleep!

A: (*Mimes being fast asleep, leaning head on hands and snoring*)

Narr: So they woke him up. . .

B: (*Shaking A*) Here, wake up! Get up and pray to your god for help!

Narr: But still the storm continued. So the sailors decided to draw lots to see who was to blame. . .

A: What's a lot?

B: About this much! (*Stretches arms wide*)

Narr: No, no! This is a lot. (*Narrator hands a piece of string or straw, first to A—who chooses the shortest piece—then to B, then to a few members of the audience*)

A: Oo errr!

B: It's you! You're the one! What have you done?

Narr: Yep! Jonah had drawn the short straw.

A: Well, you know God, who created everything including the sea and the land?

B: Nope!

A: Well, I do, and I'm trying to escape from him!

Narr: The sailors were terrified!

B: Fancy trying to escape from a god who created everything! What are we going to do?

Narr: So Jonah said, 'Throw me into the sea, and it will calm down. I know it's my fault that you're caught in this violent storm.'

A: We can't do that!

B: It's against our better nature!

Narr: So they tried to row to the shore. . .

A and B: (*Mime rowing with all their might*)

Narr: But the storm was getting worse and worse.

B: We're sorry, Lord, there's only one thing for it—please don't punish us for taking this man's life.

Narr: And they threw Jonah into the sea.

A and B: S P L A S H ! Glug, glug, glug!

Narr: And the sea calmed down at once.

B: G U L P !

A: Yuck! Where am I? (*Sniffs*) There's something fishy going on here. Hang on a mo! I've been swallowed by a fish! A big gloopy fish! Yuck!

Narr: God had sent a big fish to rescue Jonah. Jonah spent three days and three nights inside that fish—thinking things through.

A: Oh, what an idiot I've been! I'm sorry, Lord. How could I have been so stupid to have thought I could run away from you? Please don't leave me here!

Narr: God heard Jonah's prayer for forgiveness and the fish began to feel a bit sick. . .

B: (*Mimes feeling sick*)

Narr: . . .it swam to the beach and there it *was* sick.

B: Yuck!

Narr: You can say that again!

B: Yuck!

Narr: So Jonah went to Nineveh and gave God's message to the people. . .

A: In forty days Nineveh will be destroyed!

Narr: And the people of Nineveh believed God's message and they turned from their wicked ways.

B: Wow!

Narr: The king of Nineveh put out a declaration to his people. . .

A: All persons and animals must wear sackcloth and pray to God.

B: Even the sheep.

A: Even the goats.

B: Even the cattle.

A: Everyone!

Narr: And God had mercy on them and did not punish them as he said he would.

A: Wow!

B: Thank you, Lord!

Narr: And that is how Jonah learnt that nothing can separate us from the love of God.

Quiz 2, memory verse recap, prayer and theme song

The Big Top

GOD'S LOVE—*Escape Artist, Jonah*

God asked these people to do a job for him.
Who said 'yes' and who said 'no'?

Find the words hidden in the big fish.

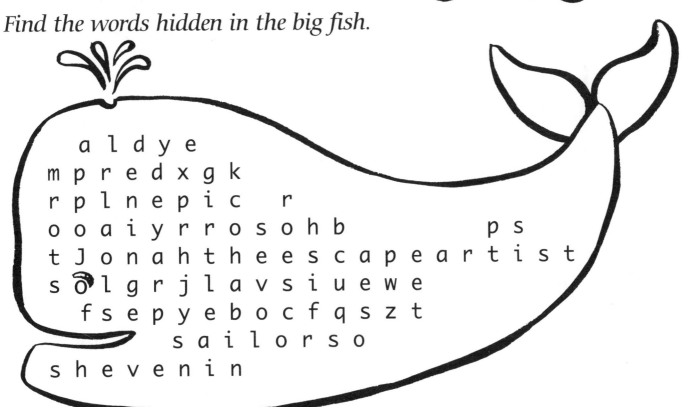

```
        a l d y e
    m p r e d x g k
    r p l n e p i c   r
    o o a i y r r o s o h b          p s
    t J o n a h t h e e s c a p e a r t i s t
    s o l g r j l a v s i u e w e
      f s e p y e b o c f q s z t
          s a i l o r s o
  s h e v e n i n
```

fish   love   obey   sailors   Joppa   Nineveh   prayed   sea   Jonah   the
escape   artist   sorry   storm

Re-arrange the words below to find today's memory verse.

long God how how is deep the broad of high how how love

___ ____, ___ ____, ___ ____, ___ ____ __ __ ___ __ ____ ___ ____.

love separate that can certain am his from I nothing us

_ __ _____ ___ _____ _ _____ __ ___ __ ___ ____.

Ephesians 3 verse 18 and Romans 8 verse 38

It was God's love that saved both Jonah and Nineveh. Colour in the words which you would use to describe God's love.

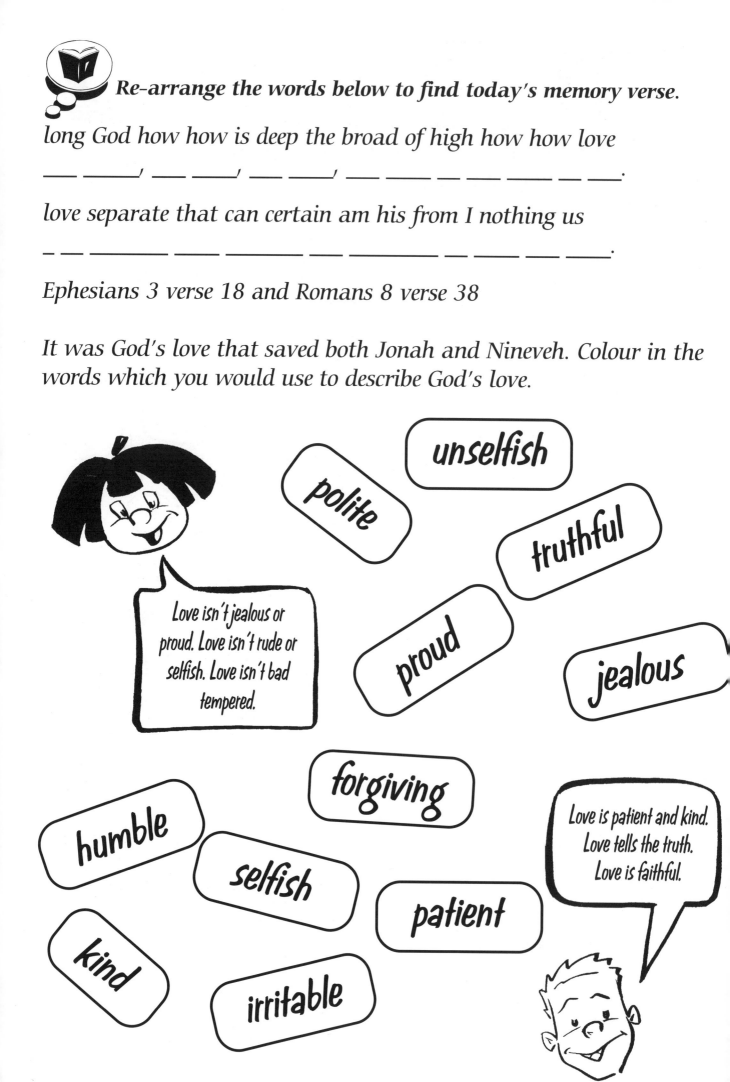

Day 3

GOD'S POWER

Fire-eater, Elijah, goes it alone for God

Aim

To show that although we may go through all sorts of problems and difficulties, when we have God as our friend we know ultimately that God's power is supreme.

Warm up

See Day 1

Theme song

See Day 1

Theme illustration

Prepare an empty two litre fizzy drink bottle, refilled right to the top with clear water. Have ready a bucket and a jug of blue water (just add food colouring). Ask the children what you have to do to get the blue water into the already full bottle. Then get a volunteer to come and empty the bottle and refill it from the jug. Explain that God wants to fill us with his Holy Spirit and his power, but sometimes we are so full of ourselves that we don't leave any room for him to get in. It's not easy to stop thinking about ourselves and start thinking about others, but the Bible says that when we feel weak and helpless, that's when God's power is more evident in us.

Drama/Adventure story

The Watt family circus adventure: III

What was Grandma Watt knitting? What amazing, new act did Rick and Wendy dream up? What did Great Uncle Waldo and the kids go off to get? What happened to Grandma Watt whilst their backs were turned? Now everyone is in total confusion. Grandma Watt has disappeared and nobody saw where she went. Can the audience remember what happened? (*Audience responds*) So Grandma Watt had been peering into the cannon, had she, when she mysteriously disappeared?

The Watt kids and Great Uncle Waldo crowd around the cannon looking for clues. Rick peers inside the mouth of the cannon, but all he finds in there is an old boot. Great Uncle Waldo looks underneath the cannon, but all he finds is an old sandwich. Wendy searches around the back of the cannon, but all she finds is a joke fish. Then Great Uncle Waldo looks under the cannon's little wheels, and there, tucked into the wheel arch is a piece of paper. What's this? A note from the hooded man!

Great Uncle Waldo reads it out. HA HA HA! YOU THOUGHT YOU COULD KEEP GOING, BUT I'VE GOT YOUR NEW ACT TOO! THERE'S NO FUTURE IN THE CIRCUS FOR YOU, WALDO WATT! I'M IN CHARGE NOW SO GIVE UP! signed 'The hooded man'.

What a to-do! Poor Great Uncle Waldo is distraught! He feels dreadfully guilty about Grandma Watt and thinks it's all his fault that she's been kidnapped. He feels powerless—he can't get his performers back and he can't find Grandma Watt. The Watt kids try to comfort him. 'Why is the hooded man being so horrid?' they ask. Great Uncle Waldo doesn't know. The Watt kids don't know what to do for the best. What are they going to do?

While they are trying to think, Whatnot is playing 'mouse' with something underneath the cannon. He is growling and trying to push his nose under the cannon, but he can't reach the object. The Watt kids go to investigate.

'What've you got there, Whatnot?' they say. What's this? There's a ball of wool underneath the cannon and the end is trailing off the stage. The Watt kids get quite excited by this discovery. What is the ball of wool doing underneath the cannon? Could it be a clue? They decide to follow the wool trail. They carefully follow the trail (*through audience, around room etc.*). At last they come to the end of the trail and what do they discover. . . Half a jumper! Newly knitted and still on the needles! Well, it could only belong to one person! Grandma Watt! But where is she? How are they ever going to find her? Just as the trail seems to have gone completely cold, Whatnot's nose begins to twitch as he sniffs at the jumper. On the back he finds a red piece of paper shaped like a fish.

'What's that, Whatnot?' cries Rick, 'Let me see, it's got some writing on it!' Is it another clue? Or just a red herring?

'What does it say?' cries Wendy. 'It's from the hooded man. It says, SO, YOU'RE STILL ON THE TRAIL OF GRANDMA, ARE YOU? IF YOU EVER WANT TO SEE HER ALIVE AGAIN YOU WILL HAVE TO ACT FAST. SHE HAS ONLY A FEW HOURS LEFT. YOU WILL FIND HER TIED UP TO A TREE IN TIMBUKTU.

'What are we going to do?' they cry. There's only one thing for it. They'll have to set off on the trail again and try to find Grandma. They disappear out of sight just as the hooded man re-appears with Grandma.

'Ha ha ha! That's them out of the way!' he laughs. Grandma hasn't taken very kindly to being kidnapped and she begins to prod the hooded man off the stage with her walking stick, telling him that he's just a naughty boy and he should stop being so silly. Soon he can take no more and disappears off stage.

Grandma sits down on stage. Just at that moment the others re-appear arguing over who was supposed to have the map. They ask Grandma if she has it. 'What do you want a map for?' she says. They start to explain and then suddenly realize that it's Grandma they're talking to! They are delighted to see her. But it doesn't solve their problem. How are they ever going to put on a show for their sell-out audience tonight? Great Uncle Waldo and the Watt kids are at their wits' end. 'Is there no other act we can get for tonight's show?' the kids ask.

'No,' says Great Uncle Waldo, 'There hasn't been a really good act for thirty years. Not since my brother, Winston Watt, who was part of the famous Watt Trapeze Team had an argument with me and walked out. We quarrelled because I wouldn't let Winston do the high-wire act without a safety net. No one's seen him since, and the Watt Trapeze Team has never been the same without him. Winston loved to perform, he loved the feeling of power that performing gave him, but it didn't do him any good in the end.'

The Watt kids feel very down-hearted. No one knows the Watt Brothers' Circus like Great Uncle Waldo—except, it seems for one person, Winston Watt. And no one knows where to find him. What are they going to do? What, what, what? Everything seemed to be going against them. YOU'LL HAVE TO WAIT UNTIL TOMORROW TO FIND OUT WHAT HAPPENED NEXT. . .

Drama/Adventure story link

It seems that all the hooded man is interested in is disrupting everything and making himself look powerful. He obviously thinks that by forcing his way it will mean that the others will give up, and he can do what he wants. When you are a Christian the idea of power is very different. If we think a lot of ourselves then God cannot do much with us. It's only when we stop forcing our way and give God a chance that he can use us to help other people in the way that is best for them—and us. That's why his 'power is made perfect in weakness'.

Memory verse

2 Corinthians 12:9. 'My grace is sufficient for you, for my power is made perfect in weakness.'

A song: The sheet music can be found in Appendix B on page 146. The song can be found on the *Ulitmate Holiday Club Guide* cassette, available from your local Christian bookshop, or, in case of difficulty, direct from BRF.

Quiz

Questions could include:

Who did Jonah try to escape from yesterday?
God

What city narrowly escaped being destroyed by God?
Nineveh

What can separate us from the love of God?
Nothing

Name one Bible reference for yesterday's memory verse
Ephesians 3:18 or Romans 8:38

Day 3: Clown power

A leader sets the scene by explaining that it's not always easy to know what to do when things seem to be going against us. We have to have a lot of courage to stick by what we know is right, even when people won't believe us. Christians often have to stick up for what they know is right about God when other people don't believe them. The leader says he knows someone who had a problem proving something which they knew was right. Let's give him a call. The leader encourages the audience to shout out for Clown B.

Clown A comes on to the stage, but Clown B isn't with him. Clown A says he heard the audience shouting for Clown B but he doesn't know where he is. Do they know? Could they help him call him? (*Audience responds*) Clown B comes on stage. Or does he? It looks like Clown B—the costume is right. But something is not quite right! (*In fact it's someone dressed in Clown B's costume and make-up, but it's not Clown B—someone physically very different from Clown B would be great*)

Clown A: (*Doesn't realize the fraud*) Hi! You're late as usual!

Impostor: (*In a deep voice*) Oh, I'm sorry!

Clown A: Pardon?

Impostor: (*Realizes the mistake and changes tone of voice to match Clown B's*) I'm sorry I'm late.

Clown A: I don't know what it is about you, but you seem different today.

Impostor: I've got a sore throat!

Clown A: Oh, is that what it is! Come on then, let's do some clowning.

(*The real Clown B wanders on to the stage at this point, wearing ordinary clothing, but with his clown make-up on.*)

Clown B: (*To Clown A*) Sorry I'm late!

Clown A: Who are you?

Clown B: What do you mean, who are you? I'm Clown B!

Clown A: Oh no you're not!

Clown B: Oh yes I am!

Clown A: Oh no you're not!

Clown B: Oh yes I am!

Clown A: No you're not!

Clown B: Yes I am!

Clown A: You're not!

Clown B: I am!

Clown A: Well, if you're Clown B, who's he? (*Points to Impostor*)

Clown B: (*Looking angry*) So that's what happened to my suit!

Clown A: What are you going on about?

Clown B: I washed my suit and put it on the line to dry. When I went to get it, it had gone!

Clown A: You don't expect me to believe such nonsense do you? You don't look like Clown B, he does! He's Clown B!

Clown B: No, he's not me! I'm me!

Clown A: No! You're not! He's you!

Clown B: Yes, I am, I'm you. . . I mean, I'm me! I'm Clown B, the clown.

Clown A: Well, I'm confused! Which of you is Clown B?

Impostor and Clown B together: I am!

Clown A: (*Looking from one to the other*) Well, you can't both be Clown B! You're going to have to prove it! (*Thinks*) Now let's see. Ah, yes! You can prove it with clown power! Let's see if you can make us laugh! You go first! (*Points to impostor*)

Impostor: (*To audience*) Oi, you lot! Laugh or else! Come on, laugh, I'm as good as he is! (*He's getting cross*)

Clown A: (*To Clown B*) Now, it's your turn.

Clown B (*Creeps up behind Impostor and steals juggling balls from his pocket. He does a juggling trick, pulls funny faces etc. and makes audience laugh*)

Clown A: Clown B, you're really you! You've got clown power, that's for sure! You've proved you're the real clown! (*To Impostor*)

You're a fake, give Clown B his clothes back!

Clown A makes Impostor take off the clown costume. Impostor slinks off stage. Clown B puts on his costume, he's delighted that Clown A recognized him at last. It's great to be a clown again! They clown around for a bit and then go off the stage together. Bye-bye everyone!

Puppets

Bert: (calling) Lucy. . . LUCY! Can you help me call Lucy, everyone? LUCY! (*Audience participation. Bert thinks he hears something and holds up hand for audience to be quiet. Listens. . .*)

Lucy: (*Snoring sound from below*)

Bert: LUCY!

Lucy: OK, I'm coming! I'm coming! (*Appears, yawning*)

Bert: You weren't still in bed, were you?

Lucy: No, I was up *very* early this morning, helping my Mum and Dad again.

Bert: Again? What were you doing this time?

Lucy: I said I would mow the lawn.

Bert: Wow! And did you?

Lucy: Well, not exactly. . .

Bert: Why not?

Lucy: 'Cos the lawnmower was broken. I had to try to fix it.

Bert: I didn't know you knew how to fix lawnmowers, Lucy!

Lucy: Nor did I! I tried fiddling with it a bit, but it still didn't work.

Bert: But it's an electric one, isn't it?

Lucy: Yes, but I couldn't find the battery.

Bert: Lucy, was there a long lead with a plug on the end?

Lucy: Yes, there was. But I didn't know what that was for.

Bert: You mean you didn't plug it in?

Lucy: Why should I do that?

Bert: Oh, Lucy, you are a banana! You won't get any power for the mower if you don't plug it in!

Lucy: So it won't work without it?

Bert: No! You have to plug it in to give it power!

Lucy: Well, how was I to know?

Bert: Come on, Lucy, let's go and see if we can

help your parents in any other way.

Lucy: OK, Bert. Bye everyone!

Bert: Bye, bye everyone—see you tomorrow!

Bible story

Elijah makes himself look weak in order to show how great God's power is. Read the account in 1 Kings 18:20–46.

Key points

Elijah set the challenge to prove who was the true God.

He was one prophet against four hundred and fifty prophets of Baal.

The challenge was to see whose god could light the sacrificial pyre.

Elijah encourages us to look beyond our normal understanding and ability, pointing to God's all-surpassing power.

Style suggestion

Cast: Narrator and two others (A and B)

Narr: Have you ever been in a situation where you know you are right about something, but everyone else disagrees with you?

A and B: *(Stand facing each other)*

A: You're wrong!

B: I'm right!

A: No! You're wrong!

B: Right!

A: Wrong!

B: Right!

A: Wrong!

B: Right!

A: Wr. . . *(To narrator)* What do you think?

Narr: *(Stands behind B and says to B)* You're wrong.

B: *(Looking at narrator)* No, I'm right!

A: Wrong!

B: *(Looking at A)* Right!

Narr: Wrong!

B: *(Looking at narrator)* Right!

A: Wrong!

B: *(Looking at A)* Right!

Narr: Wrong!

B: Wrong!. . . Oh! I'm confused!

Narr: That happens very easily when you're outnumbered. It's easier just to follow the crowd. There was a man in the Bible who knew he was right. But there were 850 people who all thought that he was wrong. His name was Elijah.

A: 850 against 1! Well, this Elijah chappie must have been wrong!

Narr: Why?

A: Because 850 people can't be wrong!

Narr: Oh yes they can! And they were most definitely wrong!

B: How's that then?

Narr: God's people, the Israelites, were confused because their king, King Ahab, had started to worship his wife's god which was an idol called Baal. He was telling all his people that they must worship the idol too.

B: Bone idle!

A: Lazy lot!

Narr: No, no! An idol is a sort of statue.

A: So the king and queen and the 850 others said that everyone should worship this Baal?

Narr: Most of them did. A few people carried on worshipping the true God. But their lives were in danger because the king's wife hunted down anyone who wouldn't worship her god.

B: Cor! What a predicament!

Narr: Elijah decided enough was enough and he challenged the king and the prophets of Baal to a contest.

A: What! He challenged them all on his own!

Narr: Yep!

B: He was a brave chap!

Narr: Yep! But he also knew that he was right! He got them all to meet him on Mount Carmel. And, when they were all gathered, he said to them. . .

A: How much longer will it take you to make up your minds? If the Lord is God, worship him; but if Baal is God, worship him!

Narr: So the prophets of Baal built an altar. It looked a bit like a bonfire with a base of stones. And Elijah did the same. Elijah used twelve stones for his base—one for each of the twelve tribes of Israel.

A: Did they have to light the fires?

Narr: No! Elijah said to them. . .

B: Pray to your god, and I will pray to the Lord. The one who answers by sending fire—he is God!

A: Hooray! What a jolly good idea!

B: After you!

A: *(Calmly)* Send the fire, Baal.

Narr: No fire.

A: *(A bit louder)* Send the fire, Baal!

Narr: Still no fire!

A: *(A starts to dance around frenetically)* Hey, Baal, SEND THE FIRE!

Narr: Still no fire! Elijah started to mock them. . .

B: Pray louder! Maybe your god is daydreaming, or in the loo! Maybe he's gone on holiday! Or perhaps he's asleep, and you've got to wake him up!

Narr: And the prophets of Baal prayed louder and worked themselves into a frenzy.

A: S E N D   T H E   F I R E ! ! *(A goes crazy)*

Narr: They carried on ranting and raving until

the middle of the afternoon; but no answer came, not a sound was heard. Then Elijah said to the people. . .

B: Come closer to me.

Narr: They gathered round him. Elijah set about repairing the altar of the Lord, which had been torn down in the frenzy.

B: (*B mimes rebuilding the stones*)

Narr: Then he dug a deep trench around the altar and said. . .

B: . . . fill four jugs with water and pour it on the offering and the wood.

A: That's the last thing you do if you're trying to light a fire!

B: Do it again!

A: Wouldn't you prefer a match?

B: And again!

A: Here that water's running everywhere! Your altar is soaking wet, mate!

Narr: Then Elijah said one small, quiet prayer to the Lord. . .

B: O Lord, the God of Abraham, Isaac, and Jacob, prove now that you are the God of Israel and that I am your servant and have done all this at your command.

Narr: And down came the fire!

A: (*Leaps back*) Ahh!

Narr: It completely destroyed the altar and scorched the ground around it.

A: (*Throws himself on the ground*)

A and B: The Lord is God; the Lord alone is God!

Narr: One little prayer to the real God is all it took. That day everyone saw the power of the Lord. Elijah hadn't followed the crowd. He knew he was right and he put his trust in the one true God.

Quiz 2, *memory verse recap, prayer and theme song*

The Big Top

***GOD'S POWER**—Fire-eater, Elijah*

Fan Elijah's flames into life with colour.

 Unscramble today's memory verse.

my rgcae si fufsecntii orf oyu, rof ym owpre si dame erpftce ni eawnesks.

M_ _'

_ _

2 Corinthians 12 verse

How many words can you make from...

ELIJAH THE FIRE-EATER.

*Can you help
the fire find
the way to
the altar?*

 *Today's memory verse talks about grace. Grace is the word
we use to describe the way God gives us what we don't
deserve.*

What is good about God's grace? _____

In what ways is it all we need? _____

How can God use us when we are weak?_____

Write your answers on the lines or draw a picture in the space below.

Day 4

GOD'S FAITHFULNESS

Lion-tamer, Daniel, faces the savage beasts

Aim

To show that we have a responsibility to stay faithful to God. Daniel was a shining example of this. Our faithfulness to God pales in comparison to God's faithfulness to us. We can be bold as we persevere in our Christian lives, knowing that God is with us.

Warm up

See Day 1

Theme Song

See Day 1

Theme illustration

This illustration relies on feedback from the children. Ask them who they liked best during the week. Was it their team leader? Or the clowns? Or Bert and Lucy? Or was it something or someone else? It's good to enjoy all the different things. We all have favourite people or things. But God loves each one of us equally. His love doesn't depend on who we are or what we do. His love is always constant and faithful. He wanted us to try to be faithful to him and to each other, and to try to show his love to other people.

Drama/Adventure story

The Watt family circus adventure: IV

What did Rick find in the mouth of the cannon? What did Wendy find behind it? What did the note from the hooded man say? What was at the end of the trail of wool? What was the act that caused Great Uncle Waldo and his brother Winston to quarrel?

Great Uncle Waldo has to make a decision. There's only a couple of hours left before the audience will start to arrive for the evening's performance. Without a show, he'll be finished. Telling the Watt kids about Winston has given him an idea. Winston's star trick used to be the greatest high-wire act ever, diving and swinging

through the air. The audience used to love his act—he used to draw a full house every time. Great Uncle Waldo decides that he will do Winston's act tonight—without the safety net! He goes away to change so that he can practise the act before the show, leaving the Watt kids sitting on the upturned barrel, talking excitedly about what Great Uncle Waldo has decided to do.

Suddenly the hooded man creeps onto the stage and stands listening to their conversation. (*Audience responds*). But the Watt kids don't see him, they are so deep in their conversation. The hooded man creeps off the stage again and disappears.

Great Uncle Waldo comes back on stage carrying a step ladder. He's changed into a trapeze artist's costume, but doesn't really look the part—he's even forgotten to take off his Big Top hat. The Watt kids think he looked much better in his ringmaster's outfit. Poor Great Uncle Waldo looks very nervous. He sets the step ladder up on the stage and starts to climb slowly up the rungs. He has just reached halfway to the top of the ladder when the hooded man suddenly rushes onto the stage and dashes over to the ladder.

'Stop!' he cries, 'It's impossible, and you know it! I can't let you do it!' Without fully hearing what he has said, Rick and Wendy rush to grab him and so begins a manic chase around the stage and the audience. At last, after several failed attempts they succeed in pinning the hooded man to the floor. With Rick and Wendy sitting on his back and Grandma pinning his shoulders down with her walking stick, Great Uncle Waldo whips off his hood and who do you think it is?

It's Winston! Great Uncle Waldo can hardly believe his eyes. He stares down at his long-lost brother.

'Winston,' he stammers, 'it's you! I don't believe it! You've come back! But why are you trying to stop me doing the act?' Winston is looking a little sheepish.

'For a long time I was really jealous of you, because you were in charge and I wanted to be', he said. 'I wanted to run the whole show and have all the power—and you wouldn't even let me do my act without a safety net! But now I know that you were right. It was too big a risk for anyone to take. It wasn't until I heard that you were going to attempt it that I suddenly knew how you felt about me doing it! I can't let you do it any more than you could let me all those years ago!'

'But, Winston,' said Great Uncle Waldo, giving his long-lost brother a hug, 'I only had your best interests at heart. I didn't want to see you hurt!'

Well, the two brothers started to work together again, and all the performers came back and the show went ahead as planned. The audience loved every single moment of it—especially the Watt Trapeze Team with Winston diving and swinging through the air—with a safety net! So the Watt Brothers have put the past behind them and they're working together again now. The Watt kids had a fantastic week, helping out at the circus. Now they have two favourite great-uncles instead of one. What a to-do! What a happy ending!

Drama/Adventure story link

What a relief! Who would have thought that after all these years, Winston would appear again! It was good that at the end of it all he was able to stay faithful to Waldo, despite the hunger for power going to his head for a while. Waldo, of course, was delighted to make up with his brother. We do our best to be faithful to those we love—and so we should. When you are a Christian you also want to be faithful to God and try to put him first. In return, God will always be faithful to you; he will never let you down.

Memory verse

2 Timothy 4:7 'I have done my best in the race, run the full distance and kept my faith.'

A song: The sheet music can be found in Appendix B on page 146. The song can be found on the *Ultimate Holiday Club Guide* cassette, available from your local Christian bookshop, or, in case of difficulty, direct from BRF.

Quiz

Questions could include:

How many prophets was Elijah up against in yesterday's story?
   850

How do you start a teddy bear race?
   Ready, teddy, go!

How do you start a jelly race?
   On your marks, get set, go!

How do you start a pudding race?
   You just sago!

Day 4: Easy as custard pie!

A leader sets the scene by explaining to the audience that things aren't always as easy as we'd like them to be. Have they every tried clowning, for instance? He gets one or two members of the audience to come on to the stage to try different tricks, juggling etc. It's not very easy, is it! Being a Christian isn't always easy. But, one thing's for sure, God will always stick with us if we stick with him. The leader says he's got some friends who've got sticking power. Let's give them a call. He encourages audience to call out for Clowns A and B.

Clown B comes on stage and starts doing some clowning with the audience. Clown A enters.

Clown A: *(To Clown B)* Is it you?

Clown B: What do you mean, is it me! Of course it's me, you narna!

Clown A: I was just checking after yesterday! Let's do some clowning together.

The two clowns do some clowning with the audience. The person who played the part of the impostor on the previous day wanders on stage.

Impostor: Hi, guys!

Clown B: Oh, it's you!

Clown A: What do you want?

Impostor: I just wanted to say that I was sorry about what happened yesterday. You see, I've always wanted to be a clown. Could you teach me?

Clown A: It takes a lot of skill, time and practice.

Impostor: It can't do! It always looks so easy!

Clown B: Well, it isn't!

Impostor: Well, I don't believe you! Prove it!

Clown A: The only way we can prove it is by teaching you. Then you'll realize.

Impostor: That's fine by me!

Clown B: I'll get the spare suit! *(Goes off and comes back with clown suit)*

Impostor: I'm not wearing that!

Clown B: Oh yes you are! *(He messes around putting trousers on impostor's head etc., until they finally get him dressed)*

Impostor: Yuck! I feel really stupid. But at least I'm a clown now.

Clown A: Oh no you're not!

Clown B: Make-up!

Impostor: No way! I'm not letting you put that stuff on my face!

Clown A: I thought you wanted to be a clown?

Impostor: I do!

Clown A: Then you'll have to wear the make-up! (*They mess around and finally get him made up*)

Impostor: Yuck, now I look really stupid! But at least I'm a clown now.

Clown A: Oh no you're not! You've got to pull faces like a clown! (*They demonstrate*) Talk like a clown! (*They demonstrate*) Juggle like a clown! (*They demonstrate*) Play tricks like a clown! (*They demonstrate*) Hey, where are you going?

Impostor: I've had enough, it's too hard.

Clown A: But we can teach you!

Clown B: It's hard work but it's worth it in the end!

Impostor: No thanks! (*He climbs out of the clown suit*)

Clown A: He's gone!

Clown B: Yeah, what a shame, he's missed out on so much!

Clown A: No sticking power! Let's do some clowning together.

They clown together for a while and then go off stage together. Bye-bye everyone!

Puppets

Bert: What's up, Lucy?

Lucy: I'm fed up.

Bert: Why?

Lucy: 'cos I am. That's why.

Bert: But why?

Lucy: Look, are you having a go at me?

Bert: No, of course not! I just want to see if there's anything I can do to help.

Lucy: Well, it just seems as though everybody is getting at me today.

Bert: Like who?

Lucy: Well, it all started at the breakfast table, when my dad told me off for playing with the lawnmower.

Bert: Well, that was a little silly.

Lucy: Don't you start! Then my brother knocked me and I spilt my cereal, so I got

told off for that. Then on my way here I ripped my trousers on my bicycle and bumped into someone—and they had a go at me too.

Bert: Oh, I'm sorry, Lucy.

Lucy: So I have expected you to start saying horrible things to me too.

Bert: But I wouldn't do that!

Lucy: Well, you may as well—everyone else has!

Bert: But I'm your friend, Lucy. You know I'll stick by you.

Lucy: Really?

Bert: Yes, really.

Lucy: What, always?

Bert: Yes, always!

Lucy: Oh, thank you, Bert! I feel a bit better all ready.

Bert: Come on, say goodbye and let's get some chocolate!

Lucy: Yeah! Bye, bye everyone!

Bert: Bye!

Bible Story

Daniel was a man of faith who clearly knew God's faithfulness in his own life. Read the account of Daniel in his book, with particular reference to the lions' den in Daniel 6:1–28.

Key Points

When Daniel's enemies tricked King Darius into signing an ungodly law, preventing worship of anyone but the king. Daniel knew his priority and kept on praying to God, despite the danger.

Breaking this law meant Daniel faced certain death in the den of lions.

Nothing is beyond God's control, and his faithfulness saved Daniel even when facing the jaws of death; it also set King Darius back on the right track and destroyed Daniel's enemies.

Daniel is faithful to God and God is faithful to Daniel.

Style suggestion

Cast: Narrator and two others (A and B)

Narr: (*To audience*) Is there anyone here who has a long first name? Has anyone got a name with more than eight letters? Ten? etc. . . There was a man in the Bible who had fourteen letters in his name!

A: Fourteen letters!

Narr: Yep! Nebuchadnezzar.

A: (*Falls around laughing*) What a funny name!

B: Neb-u-chad-nezzar.

A: Hi, Nebby!

B: Nebbs, how you doin' man?! (*They smack hands in greeting*)

Narr: But you didn't take the mickey out of

him! He was the most powerful man in the whole world. He was the most powerful king, with the strongest army and the greatest empire! He attacked other empires and other countries and took his prisoners to work as slaves.

A: To work in the fields.

B: To work on the building sites.

Narr: And some to work in the king's palace as trainee wise men! These men had to be from noble families.

A: Handsome!

B: And intelligent!

Narr: The king ordered his chief official to select some young men from amongst the Israelite's noble families.

A goes down into audience and start selecting a few people to go up onto stage.

A: Right, you lot. Help me choose. Who's handsome round here? Who's brainy?

A makes selection by asking silly questions and making jokey comments.

A: What's the square root of 10? Wrong, it's 3.1623! etc. . .

Narr: It was a hard test to pass, but Daniel and some of his friends did pass, and they went and lived in the palace.

A brings a few people on stage. B joins them.

Narr: Although they were still slaves, they were far better off than anyone else. At meal times they ate food fit for a king and most of them tucked in. . .

A: (*Hands out sweets to people on stage*) Yum, yum!

B: Excuse me, I can't eat this food.

A: But the king has decided what you eat and if you get skinny he'll have me killed!

B: Don't worry, just give me vegetables, I'll be fine.

Narr: So that's what they did. And Daniel stayed fit and healthy.

A: My, you're a healthy lad! Off you go, you lot, Daniel's going to be a member of my court! (*Members of audience leave stage*)

Narr: Many years went by.

A: Many, many years!

B: Many, many, many years!

Narr: Nebuchadnezzar died and his son became king.

A: Many years went by.

B: Many, many, years!

A: Many, many, many years!

Narr: And that king died and a foreign king took over; his name was Darius.

A: Daniel was now very old.

B: Very, very old!

A: Very, very, very old!

Narr: King Darius heard how wise Daniel was, and he chose him to be his Prime Minister. This made all the other wise men very jealous.

A: Fancy choosing him!

B: It's not fair!

A: He's just a slave!

B: We've got to get rid of him!

A: Yeah! (*They plot together*)

Narr: So they watched to see if he would do anything wrong so they could turn the king against him.

A: He hasn't done anything wrong!

B: How can we get him?

A: I know, we'll get him through his God! He prays three times a day to his God. . .

Narr: So they went to the king. . .

A: King Darius, may your majesty live for ever!

B: We think you are so great that everyone should worship you and you alone for thirty days!

A: Anyone who disobeys should be thrown to the lions!

B: Roar!

Narr: Weren't they creeps! But the king fell for it and signed the law they had written. A few days later they went back to the king. . .

A: King Darius, may your majesty live for ever!

B: Someone has broken your law!

A and B: D A N I E L !

Narr: When the king heard this, he knew that they had tricked him. He tried hard to think of something to save Daniel, but he couldn't find a way.

A: We've got him!

Narr: So the king had to have Daniel arrested. He was to be thrown into the pit of lions.

B: May your God, whom you serve so loyally, rescue you, Daniel.

Narr: A stone was put over the entrance to the lion's pit.

A: (*Dances round gleefully*) That's him out of the way!

Narr: The king couldn't sleep all night. First thing in the morning he got up and hurried to the pit. When he got there he called out anxiously. . .

B: Daniel, servant of the living God! Was the God you serve so loyally able to save you from the lions?

A: May your majesty live for ever! God sent his angel to shut the mouths of the lions so that they would not hurt me!

Narr: The king was overjoyed. He gave orders for Daniel to be pulled out of the pit. Then he had the men who had accused Daniel arrested and thrown in instead.

A: God didn't rescue them!

Narr: King Darius commanded that everyone throughout his empire should serve Daniel's God—the one true God.

A: All through his life Daniel followed God!

B: He knew that God could be trusted and was always faithful!

Quiz 2, memory verse recap, prayer and theme song

The Big Top

***GOD'S FAITHFULNESS*—Lion-tamer, Daniel**

Find the path to Daniel.

 Unscramble the words of today's memory verse and put them in the right order.

care ym node vahe aifth pekt cantisde lufl steb ni hte I nur het nad ym

I ____ ____ __ ____ __ ___ ____,

_ ____ ___ ___ ____ _____ ___ ____ ___ _____.

2 Timothy 4 verse 7

Colour the picture of King Darius looking into the lions' den.

Choose a word which shows how Daniel was faithful to God. P____

Choose a word which shows how God was faithful to Daniel. P_____

Choose a word which shows how we can be faithful to the people who care for us. K___

Choose a word which shows how we can be faithful to our friends. L____

Choose a word which shows how we can be faithful to God. L____

prayed
silent
kind
loyal
loving
mean
rude
ignore
lift
slept
forgot
protected
selfish
wrong

Day 5
GOD'S LEADERSHIP

Ringmaster, Moses, knows who's really in charge

Aim

To show that when God asked Moses to lead the Israelites to the Promised Land, Moses didn't think he was up to it, but he soon found out that with God's help anything is possible.

Warm up

See Day 1

Theme song

See Day 1

Theme illustration

Set up a tray of objects, such as you would for Kim's game, with a wide variety of interesting things. Have one or two that seem especially attractive, such as coin or a bar of chocolate. Also, on the tray, have prepared an old used envelope, a bit screwed up, with either a voucher or money inside.

Pick a volunteer, perhaps someone whose birthday is nearest that day. Ask them to call out the items on the tray. Then put the tray out of sight and ask everyone to recall as many items as they can. Finally ask them to pick one that they would like to keep (usually the coin or the chocolate). Bring out the point that we can only remember or know so much, but God knows everything about us.

Show the tray again, saying that we don't know and see *everything* when we make choices. We do so only based on what we understand. But God chooses with a far greater level of understanding and insight. Reveal what was inside the screwed up envelope and bring out the point that when God chooses people to do a job he picks them for what he sees on the inside, not on the outside. Moses might have been just an old shepherd, but God knew the trust and potential that he had.

Drama/Adventure story

The Watt family circus adventure: V

Great Uncle Waldo and the Watt family appear for a final time. They explain that life in the circus is very exciting. Life as a Christian can be exciting too. We need to be strong, to try to do the things we know to be right and to practise the things we are good at so that we

can use them to make other people happy. When we let him, God helps us to get the best out of life. Just as the people in the circus have a skill that they are especially good at, so God gives each of us skills that we can use to do good things— sometimes things we never imagined we could do!

Being a Christian is actually all about love. It means putting the needs of others first, and showing our love for them by what we do. Wendy, Rick and Grandma Watt were prepared to do anything (well, almost!) to help Great Uncle Waldo. Jesus was prepared to do much much more to help us—for him that meant dying on the cross so that we can be friends with God for ever. That's a very special kind of love. The hooded man's idea of how to get power was actually opposed to God's rules. God says that he can only work in our lives when we accept that we are weak. I bet the hooded man didn't think of that!

It all worked out in the end, though. Waldo and Winston realized that things worked better when they worked together. God wants us to do our best, but it's not a competition to see who can *be* the best—we all have an equal part to play in making God's world a happy place. And God is here to help us as we live our lives for him. Being a Christian is an adventure that goes on long after the circus has left town!

Memory verse

Matthew 28:20 'I will be with you always, to the end of the age.'

A song: The sheet music can be found in Appendix B on page 146. The song can be found on the *Ultimate Holiday Club Guide* cassette, available from your local Christian bookshop, or, in case of difficulty, direct from BRF.

 ### Quiz

Questions could include:

What does it say in 2 Timothy 4:7?
'I have done my best in the race, run the full distance and kept my faith.'

Why was Lucy fed up yesterday?
Because everyone was having a go at her.

Who had fourteen letters in his name?
Nebuchadnezzar.

How did Daniel sleep in the lion's den?
Lion down.

Clowns

When you think you can't do something it makes all the difference when someone who can do it comes along to help you.

Clown A: Hi everyone *(looking sad)*

Clown B: Hi you all, it's great to see you! Hi... *(he names Clown A)*

Clown A: I'm sad.

Clown B: Sad? Why?

Clown A: 'Cos my teeth are playing me up.

Clown B: What? Have they been cheeky to you?

Clown A: No, don't be daft! I've got toothache.

Clown B: *(Get's the audience to say 'Aaah')* Let's have a look. *(He yanks open Clown A's mouth.)*

Clown A: Ouch!! Be careful!

Clown B: You should see a dentist!

Clown A: No way! NEVER!! They hurt you.

Clown B: Your teeth will get worse if you don't. You may end up with teeth like mine... *(he produces 'joke' chattering teeth).*

Clown A: *(Screams loudly)* Oh, it was a joke—not a very funny one.

Clown B: You should go to the dentist. Have you brushed your teeth today?

Clown A: Er... no—they hurt too much.

Clown B: Tut, tut, tut!

Clown A: Em... I lost my toothbrush.

Clown B: I've got a spare one. *(He produces a broom.)*

Clown A: Ha, ha, ha, very funny! Are you trying to say I've got a big mouth?

Clown B: *(Produces an ordinary toothbrush)* Here's a proper one—I know something that will cheer you up... *(He gives Clown A a pair of sunglasses and puts on his own.)*

Clown B: Listen! *(he starts a rap beat.)*

If you don't brush your teeth you'll be in lots of trouble;
Especially if you eat lots of sweets and bubble (gum!).
So the dentist is the place to go;
You'll have strong teeth that you'll want to show. *(smiles)*
So don't be afraid and do not fear;
'Cos wherever you go, I'll be near!

Clown A: What did you say?

Clown B: I'll be near.

Clown A: I thought so. Do you mean you'll come with me?

Clown B: Yes, of course. I know the dentist can be a scary place - so I'll come with you.

Clown A: Great! Thanks! Let's go! It makes all the difference when someone is with you!

Moses didn't want to be the one to lead the people of Israel out of Egypt, but he was able to do it because God promised to be with him.

Puppets

(Puppets come up arguing)

Lucy: No way, that's not fair!

Bert: Come on, Lucy, stop being silly.

Lucy: I'm not, you're the one being silly.

Bert: Me? I'm not!

Lucy: But I want to do it.

Bert: Lucy, you can't even juggle one ball, let alone three eggs!

Lucy: So. I'll just do it my way.

Bert: Yeah? Well, they'll smash. Then what'll your mum and dad say?!

Lucy: But Bert, you always said you'd teach me how to juggle.

Bert: Exactly. But not here, and not with eggs!

Lucy: But I want to.

Bert: Lucy, you and I can go and practise first.

Lucy: But it's much better to do it now. Come on, it's not fair. Let me do it.

Bert: Well, if you're going to make that much of a fuss, go on then. But don't come running to me if it they all go splat!

Lucy: It'll be fine, thank you very much. Right, watch everybody! *(Pauses)* Well... just a minute... er... Bert?

Bert: Yes, Lucy?

Lucy: I was just starting but now I'm not sure... maybe... er... could you help me? Please?

Bert: Yes, silly, course I can! Let's go and find some real juggling balls.

Lucy: Yeah... OK! And some eggs!

Bert: Next time, folks, we'll have Lucy and the incredible flying eggs... say Bye bye, Lucy...

Lucy: Bye bye, Lucy...

Bert: Bye bye, everyone!

Bible Story

Moses knows who's really in charge. The story is based on Exodus 3.

Key points

● *Moses had had quite an eventful life so far, in fact he was now in his eighties.*

● *Although he lacked confidence in himself, God chose to use him.*

● *God spoke to him through a burning bush in the middle of the desert.*

● *Moses was anxious about what God wanted him to do.*

● *God promised to be with him and to help him.*

● *Moses learnt to put his trust in God and because of that he became a great leader.*

Style suggestion

Cast: Narrator and two others (A and B)

Narr: Sometimes we're asked to do something we don't want to do…

A: (*Calls to B*) Can you do the washing up?

B: Huh! No way! Do it yourself!

Narr: … and sometimes we might be asked to do something we feel is too hard for us…

A: (*Calls to B*) Can you make a cake for me?

B: Who me?

A: Yes, you!

B: I can't do that!

A: Why?

B: Because I wouldn't know what to do—it's too hard!

B: (*Calls to A*) Can you sing a solo with me in the school assembly tomorrow?

A: I can't do that!

B: Why?

A: Because there are lots of people—and I can't sing!

Narr: There was a man in the Bible who God chose to do a special job. He asked him to be the leader of a lot of people—a bit like a ringmaster!

A: But although he knew the job was very important…

B: He also knew that it would be very difficult.

Narr: He was sure that the job would suit someone who was young, brave and full of confidence—and this man was none of these!

A: In fact, he was old. He was very old, very, very, very old. Very, very, very, very… (*Others give him a nudge*).

B: And he had already run away once!

Narr: One day, as he was leading his sheep across the desert, he noticed a bush on fire.

A: So? He was in a very, very, very hot desert—I bet that sort of thing happened all the time!

Narr: Yes, but this was different. The bush wasn't actually burning up! So he decided to take a closer look, when suddenly…

A: MOSES! MOSES!

B: Don't be daft, bushes don't talk!

Narr: This one did—or at least it seemed to! Well, it was actually God—he used the bush to get Moses' attention.

A: Take off your sandals, because you are standing on holy ground.

Narr: So Moses did as God said…

A: I have seen how cruelly my people are being treated in Egypt.

Narr: God went on to talk to Moses about how his people were slaves…

B: … and how he had decided to rescue them…

A: To give them their own land, rich and fertile.

Narr: Moses must have been dancing for joy! Yes, at last!

B: God was going to set his people free!

A: I am sending you, Moses, to the king of Egypt so that you can lead my people out of his country.

B: Pardon?

Narr: Moses' face dropped.

B: Who me?

A: Yes, you!

B: To the king of Egypt?

A: YES!

Narr: Moses was terrified!

B: But I am nobody!

A: 'I will be with you' said God.

Narr: Moses made all the excuses he could think of…

B: Who shall I say sent me?

A: Say 'The one who is called I AM has sent you'.

B: (*Very scared*) B..b..b..b..but I..I..I..I s..s..s..st..st..stutter!

A: Who gives man his mouth? I will help you speak, and I will tell you what to say.

Narr: But Moses still tried to wriggle out of it…

B: No, Lord, please send someone else.

A: I don't blame him, I would have done the same! Why didn't God choose a younger, braver man?

Narr: Because God loves to use people who know that by themselves they can't do it, people who realize they need God to help them. He knows that people are happiest when their leaders are humble and good and kind, not clever and powerful—and unkind!

B: So did Moses go back to his sheep?

Narr: No, he didn't. He went to the king of Egypt, and with God's help he set the people free from slavery. He learnt what it meant to put his trust in God. Because of that, he became a great leader—and God never left him.

Quiz 2, memory verse recap, prayer and theme song

Drama workshop/Crafts display

You may wish to consider an alternative to the previous day's system of rotation. This could give you space to prepare material for a Family Service, hold a drama workshop, or create a special craft display.

The Big Top

GOD'S LEADERSHIPS—*Ringmaster, Moses*

Help Moses to find the way to the burning bush.

Colour in today's memory verse.

I will be with you always, to the end of the age

Matthew 28 verse 20

Can you spot ten differences between the two pictures?
When you've found them colour in the pictures.

Who me? I stutter! I'm a nobody! Please send someone else!

Across
1. Moses thought he was a _____.
3. God said his name was _ _.
5. Moses was looking after the _____.
9. God had heard the
   Israelites ___ out.
10. God heard the cry of his _____.

Down
2. The ____ was burning.
4. God would _____ his people.
6. Moses was to lead the people
   out of ____.
7. Moses was leading his flock
   across the _____.
8. God told Moses to take off his
   sandals because the ground was ___.

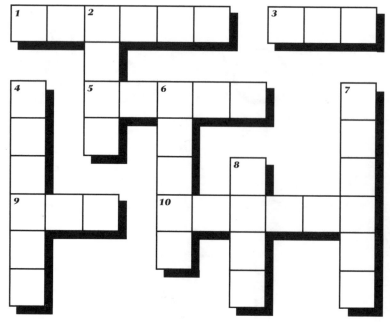

Theme 3: Starship Discovery

Setting up

Choose space names and appropriate dress for your leaders and assistants. You'll need craft leaders and sports crew to lead crafts and games, a captain to oversee sessions and crew members to assist with general running of sessions. Choose team colours and names to match the theme. Decorate your venue in keeping with the theme. The stage could be made to look like a control deck, which is easily achieved by sticking a variety of household junk on to your backdrop and spraying it silver. The rest of the room will soon be transformed with a few rolls of silver foil and as many flashing lights as you can muster.

Overview

Starship Discovery introduces us to Peter. Each day we look at a different characteristic that is illustrated by Peter's life which we can learn from today. We discover, first of all, that there is a personal choice involved when it comes to following Jesus; to turn from our old ways. On Day 2 we learn that after turning to Jesus we need to learn to trust him with all our heart. Day 3 sees Peter making mistakes. We all trip up at some stage in our lives, but God is gracious and helps us to get back on the right track. On Day 4 we see a transformation in Peter as he is equipped by God to do great things. Finally, we see Peter released from prison, and we discover our need to keep on training.

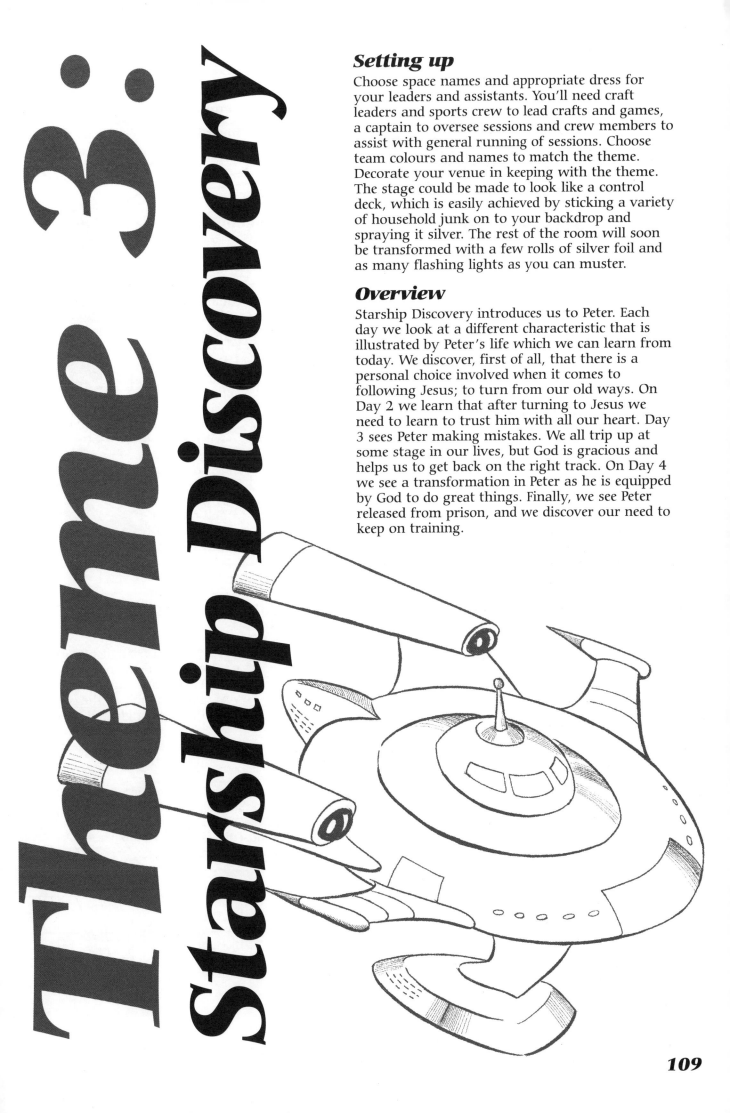

Crafts

Kaleidoscopes

For each child you will need:

Translucent sequins

One mirror-board, 16 cm x 22 cm (or foil stuck to card)

Strong card

Black sugar-paper

Greaseproof or tracing paper

Sticky tape

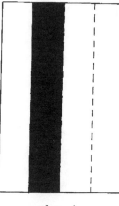

1. Score mirror-board to make four equal sections, each 4 cm wide, and cover one section in black paper.

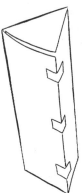

2. Fold mirror-board into a triangular prism, overlapping two sections. Hold in place with sticky tape.

3. Cover one end of triangular prism with cling film and fix into position with sticky tape.

4. Place four translucent sequins onto the cling film and cover with greaseproof or tracing paper.

5. Cut a triangle of card 4 x 4 x 4 cm and cover with black sugar-paper. Punch a hole in the centre of the triangle and fix to open end of the triangular prism, using sticky tape.

6. Cover outside of kaleidoscope with black sugar-paper.

7. As kaleidoscope is turned patterns will change.

Backpack oxygen bottles

For each child you will need:

Two clean 2-litre plastic bottles with labels removed

Red, orange and yellow crepe paper

Strips of fabric for straps

Two large elastic bands

Sticky paper labels

Masking tape

1. Strap the two bottles together with masking tape.

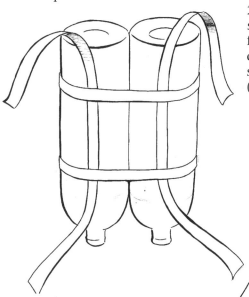

2. Cut strips of fabric to fit over child's shoulders (straps).

3. Write out labels—oxygen, food, water, Jesus, Bible, prayer etc. Stick on to bottles with the bottom of the bottle uppermost. Make flames with crepe paper and affix to neck of bottles. Fix the straps to the bottles with the elastic bands.

Memory verse rockets

For each child you will need:

One small cardboard tube

Strong card

Felt tipped pens

Aluminium cooking foil

Plain sticky label

Glue

Stapler

Sticky tape

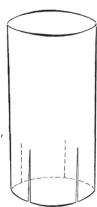

1. Cut four slits in base of tube, 5 cm deep.
2. Cut 'rocket fins' (below) out of strong card.
3. Cut slits in rocket fins as indicated.

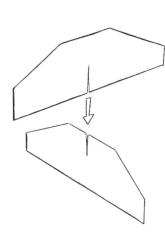

4. Interlock fins.
5. Slip fins onto rocket tube.
6. Cut a circle of card, 5 cm radius; cut out a wedge and form into cone to fit over top of rocket tube.
7. Glue or tape cone to rocket top.
8. Cover whole rocket with aluminium foil.
9. Write memory verse on sticky label and stick on rocket fins.

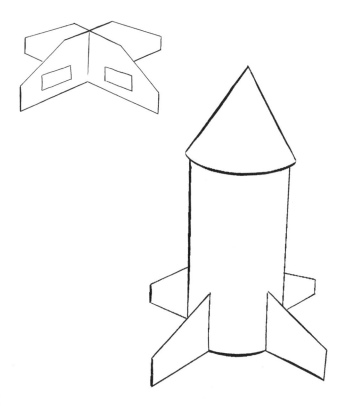

Breakthrough spinners

For each child you will need:

Two strong card circles, 15 cm diameter

Felt tipped pens

Glue

One pencil

1. Draw a picture of Peter on one card circle, placing him off centre to the left.
2. Draw a picture of Jesus on the other card circle, also placing him off centre to the left.
3. Colour in both pictures, giving them a dark background against lighter characters.
4. Glue the two circles together, sandwiching the top of the pencil between them.
5. Spin the pencil between your hands. The characters will appear to be together.

Salt dough stars

For each child you will need:

For the salt dough: 4 cups plain flour, 4 cups salt, water to mix

Small rolling-pin

Star-shaped cutter

Buttonhole thread

1. Mix ingredients and knead to form dough.
2. Roll dough flat and cut out star shape.
3. Make small hole in top of one of the star's points.
4. Place dough in a low oven until hardened.
5. Paint star.
6. Thread buttonhole thread through hole to form loop for hanging.

Starship pictures

For each child you will need:

One paper plate

Scissors

White cartridge paper

Ribbon

Felt tipped pen

Glue

Sticky tape

1. Photocopy or trace the starship picture on to the cartridge paper.
2. Colour in picture.
3. Decorate the fluted edge of the plate with shooting stars, etc.
4. Stick the picture in the middle of the paper plate.
6. Affix a loop of ribbon to the back of the plate with sticky tape to form a hanger.

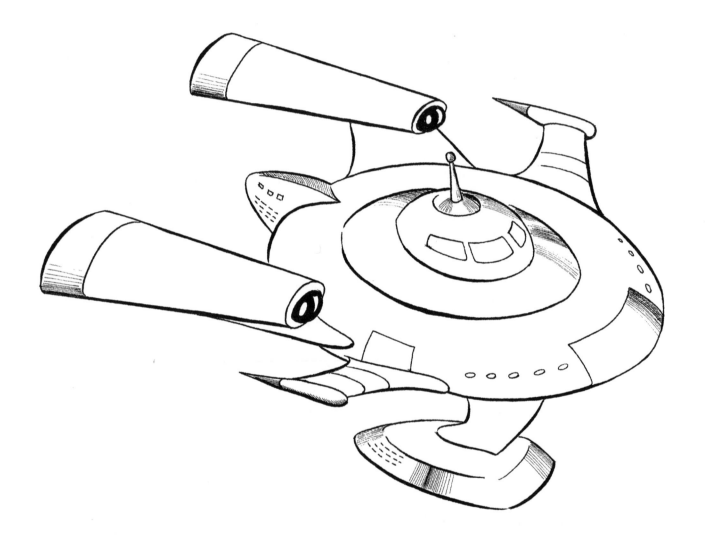

Badges

See page 33 of the Adventure Cruise theme.

Frieze

See page 33 of the Adventure Cruise theme.

Games

Stargazers

Designate a corner of the room as a black hole. Choose a leader to be the red dwarf and occupy the black hole. The caller calls out the following commands to the children, who are the stargazers:

Shooting stars Run around the room

Star dusters Pretend to dust the room

Starfish Pretend to swim around the room

Star turn Spin round

Superstars Wave your hands in the air

Starbursts Jump up and down

Star fruit Pretend to eat

Red dwarf The red dwarf comes out of the black hole to catch a stargazer and takes them back to the black hole, where they must stay until the end of the game. The last star gazer to be caught wins the game.

Musical countdown

The children dance round while music is being played. When the music stops the children freeze their poses. The leaders come round and try to make them smile whilst counting down from ten to zero. Anyone who moves or laughs is out.

Meteorites

Split the group into teams of three or four. Each team stands in a line. Place a saucer of dried peas on the floor in front of each team and an empty saucer at the back of each team line. Give each team member a straw. Each person must take turns to suck a pea onto the end of the straw and run with it to the other saucer. The team which transfers the most peas in a limited time wins the game.

Red Dwarf

Split the group into equal teams. Place a chair for each team at the far end of the room and line the teams up at the other end. Each team member has to grip hold of their ankles and run up the hall, around the chair and back to their team. When they get back they tag the next person, and so on.

Star clusters

The group dances around the room to music. When the music stops the leader shouts out a number (e.g. four) and everyone has to form a group of that number. Those who don't manage to form the right numbered group are out of the game.

Star attraction

Half the group sit on chairs in a circle, facing in. The other half of the group stand behind the people sitting on the chairs. Leave one chair empty, but have someone standing behind it. The person standing behind the empty chair invites one of the sitters to come and sit in the empty chair by winking at them. That person must then try to get up and run to the empty chair before the person standing behind them can stop them. The stopper can only restrain the sitter by placing their hands on the sitter's shoulders. If the sitter succeeds in getting away, the person standing behind the newly vacated chair then becomes the one to wink.

Day 1

  BLAST OFF—Turning; Peter chooses to follow Jesus.

 Joshua 24:15 'Choose yourself today whom you will serve; as for me, I will serve the Lord.'

 Looking at the story of Peter, we can see how each of us needs to make our own choice when it comes to following Jesus. It's not a short-term choice, but one which affects us for the rest of our lives.

Day 2

  BEAM ME UP—Trusting; Peter walks on the water.

Proverbs 3:5 'Trust in the Lord with all your heart and lean not on your own understanding.'

  Peter's trust took a big step in today's story, although he wasn't so sure afterwards! Following Jesus isn't always easy, and we have to learn to trust him, whatever our situation.

Day 3

 BLACK HOLE—Tripping; Peter's denial (and the message of the cross).

1 Timothy 1:15 'Christ Jesus came into the world to save sinners.'

 Peter was determined to be the first and best at everything, but even he tripped up in today's story. We all make mistakes, but God still loves us. Jesus showed us how much God loves us when he died on the cross. We can be friends with God, even though we all trip up.

Day 4

 BREAKTHROUGH—Transforming; Peter is transformed.

Joshua 1:5 'I will always be with you; I will never abandon you.'

 When Peter and the disciples received the Holy Spirit they were transformed by a power which changed their lives. We can know that same power when we let God work in our lives.

Day 5

 BATTLE STATIONS—Training; Peter's release from prison.

 2 Corinthians 4:8–9 'Sometimes we are troubled, but not crushed; sometimes we're in doubt, but never in despair. There are many enemies, but we always have a friend; although badly hurt at times we are not destroyed.'

 Despite being in prison, Peter knew that he was doing the right thing. We may not get put in prison for what we believe, but we need to keep in training by doing the right thing so that when things get hard we can keep going.

Day 1

BLAST OFF

Turning; Peter chooses to follow Jesus

Aim

To show that choosing to follow Jesus is a big decision. We have to leave our old self behind. It's not a short-term choice, but one which affects us for the rest of our lives.

Warm up

Choose your favourite space theme music, perhaps the Star Trek theme, and stretch to the far reaches of the galaxy, first with one hand, then with the other. Reach for the stars! Now flop over and touch your toes. Do a backwards version of 'heads and shoulders': Toes and knees, shoulders, heads. And reach right up as far as you can go. Try speeding it up, slowing it down and missing out the vital words.

Theme song

The theme song is 'Up there, out of this world'. The sheet music can be found in Appendix B on page 146. The song can be found on the *Ultimate Holiday Club Guide* cassette, available from your local Christian bookshop, or, in case of difficulty, direct from BRF.

Theme illustration 1

Prepare a cereal variety pack in advance by emptying the contents out of all but one and refilling the others with a selection of different 'surprises' such as sweets, dried lentils, scraps of paper, a balloon, 10p etc. Leave one empty. Display the packs and ask the children if they have seen the advert where the young lad finds it impossible to choose which one to have. Remind them that we all face choices every day, some big and some small. When we make decisions, it doesn't always turn out the way we expect. Invite members of the audience to come up and choose a pack. Get the volunteers to reveal their contents, ending up with the unopened pack. Today's theme is TURNING and later in the story we will meet someone who turned and made a choice which turned out to be more than he expected. Bring out the point that we need to turn and choose to follow Jesus. Then we can face all of life's unexpected surprises together.

Theme illustration 2

Two people sit as if in a car: a driver and a navigator. The navigator is holding a large map,

the driver peering intently over the wheel.

Navigator: Slow down, it's the next left… ahh, you've missed it! Turn round and go back…

Driver: No, it's all right, we'll take the next left instead.

Navigator: But it's the wrong road!

Driver: It's a nice fast road!

Navigator: But it's the wrong road!

Driver: How do you know? Look! There's lots of other traffic on this road!

Navigator: But it's the wrong road!

Driver: It's a very beautiful road. Nice views!

Navigator: But it's the wrong road!

Driver: How do you know??!

Navigator: 'Cos the map says so!

Driver: Well, we don't need a map! (*Grabs map and throws it out of window*) We're doing just fine! (*Pause*) Ahh, there's a dead end ahead! We're going in the wrong direction! Help! (*Screeches to a halt*) Now, where's that map?

Drama/Adventure story

The final frontier: 1

This is a four-part contemporary story which picks up the teaching for the week, revealing it in daily installments. The story outline can be adapted to be performed as a drama, a dramatized narration, or read as a story. Feel free to embellish and adapt the outline to suit your own situation. Play the Watt Family theme tune as the cast come on stage and again at the end of the drama (see Appendix B, page 146, also on cassette, see page 160).

Cast: **Computer**—*the narrator and mainframe support to the cast*

Rick Watt—*an untidy, adventure-mad and headstrong young lad*

Wendy Watt—*Rick's talkative and slightly annoying sister*

Mummy Watt—*keeps everything, and everyone, shipshape and in order*

Grandma Watt—*agile, yet eccentric; Amazingly scatty for someone so wise*

To set the stage for the drama, you need a space ship-style control panel. This could be made out of boxes suitably painted to look like 'the real thing'. It adds an exciting dimension if you can create your own teleport. To do this you will need three sheets of perspex, 60cm x 200cm, and a few bits of wood. Form housing, 60cm square, at the back of your set on which to build the teleport and attach the perspex on the three outwardly visible sides, using one as a door. The rear, fourth side, requires a black curtain allowing you to slip through unseen by the audience. To make your character disappear/appear you will need to hire a smoke machine, which needs to be positioned in the base of the teleport, preferably out of sight.

This will need its own operator, who can fill the teleport with smoke at the appropriate moment. For added effect install a flashing light.

Computer: Space. . . it's really big out there. This is the computer's log of the Starship Discovery, star date. . . Our mission: to explore the distant reaches of the universe and to seek out a planet as yet undiscovered by Jeremiah Beagle. The computers on board ship have been scanning a planet known as Earth to find a crew suitable for such a mission. All data received has been input and analysed. A suitable crew was found, but unfortunately they were busy, so we got. . . The Watt Family!

Chosen for this special mission, for his youthful energy, modern approach and his skill at telling awful jokes is. . . Rick Watt! As you can see, he's a nintendo sort of chap—yes, we

were looking for the ideal pilot, but Rick'll have to do.

Rick: Cor, look at all this! Wow! What does this do? Where's the start button?

Computer: Don't touch that! Leave it alone!

Rick: (*Spinning round*) Who said that? Wendy is that you?

Computer: Chosen for her intelligence, her linguistic skills—that means she talks a lot—and her amazing insight, our communications officer. . . Wendy Watt!

Wendy: Oooo, very nice!

Rick: Hey, Wendy, come and look at this. . .

Wendy: Don't touch any buttons, you might do something silly. . .

Computer: Chosen for her excellent skills in domestic engineering—that means she's a good cook, a nifty cleaner and has the ability to keep things ship-shape—as we say in computer terms, a DTP—a Drastically Tidy Person—Mummy Watt!

Mum: Oh Rick! I've found you at last. I've been looking for you. You haven't made your bed yet this morning, and your bedroom's a tip and you've left washing powder all over the kitchen floor and orange peel in the hearth and. . . (*Breaks off*) My goodness, what a mess this place is, I'll have to get it cleaned up. (*She starts dusting*)

Computer: Now, to cap it all, the brains behind the mission, bringing wisdom and experience to the crew, with crystal clear sense of direction and the ability to out-knit any challenger. . . Grandma Watt!

Grandma: Has anybody seen my cup of tea?

Computer: Assume positions ready for take off. Ten—nine—eight—seven—six—five—four—three—two—one—BLAST OFF!

As the Starship Discovery takes off, Grandma knits and natters to Rick, whose driving bears a close

resemblance to someone playing a computer game. Mum is busy cleaning and humming to herself. Wendy is pestering everyone with inane conversation.

Wendy: Slow down, Rick. Are you sure you're going the right way?

Mum: (*Wanders over to the teleport to clean it*) What a mess!

Rick: I know what I'm doing, Wendy. Stop interfering. Turn on the space TV, will you, I want to see when. . . (*Current TV programme*) is on.

Wendy: That's all you ever think about! (*She presses teleport button, thinking it's the space TV. Mum disappears.*)

Rick: Well, if you can't be bothered to turn on the TV for me, make yourself useful and go and ask Mum what's for lunch. I'm starving.

Wendy: Where's she gone? Hey, has anyone seen Mummy Watt? (*Audience participation*)

Computer: You have transported your mother to the enemy ship, Tarragon.

Wendy: Oh no I haven't!

Computer: Yes, you have! You activated the teleport while she was cleaning it.

Wendy: Oh, I thought that switch operated the TV!

Grandma: Don't panic! Don't panic! (*Everyone panics*)

Rick: How can we save her?

Wendy: Will we ever see her again?

Grandma: Who will keep Rick and Wendy out of trouble?

Rick and Wendy: Who will keep Grandma under control?

Computer: But, most of all, who will cook the dinner? YOU'LL HAVE TO WAIT UNTIL TOMORROW TO FIND OUT WHAT HAPPENS NEXT. . .

Drama/Adventure story link

Whatever next—Wendy Watt made a bad choice when it came to pressing that button. Will Mummy Watt be all right? The computer made some funny choices with all the Watt family, but he seemed to know what he was doing. Our lives are full of choices, too. Some simple, some tricky. The most important choice we'll ever make is whether or not to follow Jesus.

Memory verse

Joshua 24:15 'Choose yourself today whom you will serve: as for me, I will serve the Lord.'

A rap: <u>Choose</u> yourselves today/<u>Whom</u> you will serve/As for me, <u>I</u> WILL SERVE THE <u>LORD</u>

(shout out last line)
Underlined type = the syllable accentuated by the beat. / = claps at the end of each bar.

The sheet music can be found in Appendix B on page 146. The song can be found on the *Ultimate Holiday Club Guide* cassette, available from your local Christian bookshop, or, in case of difficulty, direct from BRF.

Quiz

Questions could include:

Why do people choose to go to bed?
Because the bed won't go to them

Why did the thief choose to take a bath?
To make a clean getaway

Where do elves choose to go to get fit?
To the elf farm

How does an intruder choose to get into a house?
Intruder window

Puppets

Lucy: I'm bored.

Bert: How d'you fancy a game of football, then?

Lucy: What, with legs like mine? (*Looks down to where legs should be*)

Bert: Aw, come on. . .

Lucy: OK, where are we going to play?

Bert: Well, outside my house there's a big wall below the railway line. It's great for a goal!

Lucy: Isn't that a bit dangerous?

Bert: Yeah, well, I often play there.

Lucy: Well, I think we should play in the park, don't you everyone? (*Audience responds*)

Bert: But there's no wall to kick against there.

Lucy: Yeah, but we could get some of our mates and play a proper match. That would be much better, wouldn't it?

Bert: But I like kicking the ball against a wall.

Lucy: Well, you know what I think, so you'll just have to choose.

Bert: Oh. . . I'm no good at making choices. I can't even decide which pair of socks to wear in the morning. (*Looks down to where legs should be again*)

Lucy: Have you got another pair like that at home? (*Looking down*)

(*Bert tries to hide fact that he's got odd socks on.*)

Lucy: Come on, Bert, you've got to choose.

Bert: Erm. . . (*To audience*) what do you lot think? (*To Lucy*) Do you really think our mates will be there?

Lucy: Well, there's only one way to find out. . .

Bert: Oh, come on then, the park it is. Bye. . .

Lucy: Bye. . .

Bible story

Peter chooses to follow Jesus. Read the three accounts in Matthew 4:18–22, Mark 1:16–20 and Luke 5:1–11.

Key Points

● *In letting down the nets at Jesus' command Peter obeyed Jesus, even though he didn't necessarily agree with him. Obedience brings results!*

● *Peter probably had already heard about Jesus, but this was the first time that Jesus had asked him to make a choice—the choice to follow him.*

● *Peter doesn't stop to weigh up the pros and cons of following Jesus; his choice is willing and immediate.*

● *Peter's choice was costly. It meant abandoning everything he knew and held dear.*

● *Peter 'left' and 'followed'. The decision is followed up by action, as in 'repent' and 'believe'.*

● *Jesus calls Peter, not just to have a passive role listening and learning from the master teacher, but to take an active role and become a 'catcher of people'.*

● *Jesus' call to Peter marks a major turning point in Peter's life. Things will never be the same again.*

Style suggestion

Cast: Narrator and two others (A and B) standing with their backs to the audience.

Narr: There was a man in the Bible who worked hard—very hard. In fact, he often worked through the night; he was a fisherman.

A and B: Turn round together and mime fishing with a fishing line.

Narr: What are you doing?

A and B: Pretending to be fishermen.

Narr: No! They didn't fish with a fishing rod like that, they had a boat with fishing nets!

A and B: Oh! (*They mime throwing nets overboard and struggle to pull the nets in.*) Cor! Look at all those fish!

Narr: Wrong! There were no fish—not that night!

A and B: (*Look fed up.*) Here, fishy, fishy, fishy! (*Keep miming casting the net, pulling it in, looking hopeful, then disappointed.*)

Narr: You won't catch any like that! They worked all through the night, but didn't catch anything.

B: Not even a goldfish?

Narr: No, not even a goldfish; it was a frustrating night. It began to get light, but their work wasn't finished yet. They pulled the boat onto the shore and started to clean their nets.

A: Cor! It was jolly hard work being a fisherman.

Narr: It certainly was! But sometimes things were much better and they would catch loads of fish, sell them and make quite a bit of money. They were quite happy being fishermen. Still, on that particular day, they'd got nothing; but as they were cleaning their nets they noticed a crowd coming along the shore. They were getting closer and closer, when suddenly a man jumped into their boat—it was Jesus!

B: Oi! Get off our boat! What a cheek, jumping into our boat like that!

Narr: No, no, no! They didn't say that! They were really pleased that Jesus had climbed onto their boat. They knew Jesus was someone special! What a guy!

A: Did he want to go fishing?

Narr: No, he wanted to speak to the crowd! He asked them if they would push the boat off a little from the shore, and then he spoke to the crowd.

B: Excellent idea! That meant he could speak to the crowd without getting soggy feet—or being pushed in!

Narr: When Jesus finished speaking, he said to Simon (one of the fishermen), 'Take your boat out to the deeper water and let your nets down for a catch.'

A: Was he a fisherman?

Narr: No, he was a carpenter!

B: Then what would he know! Cheek! They had already fished all night!

Narr: That's what Simon said, 'We've fished all night and caught nothing!' But then he added, 'Seeing as it's you, Jesus. . .' And off they went.

A and B: Come on then! (*They mime throwing the net overboard, looking a bit fed up. Then suddenly their expressions change and they struggle to pull the fish in.*) HELP!! WE'RE SINKING!! HELP!!

Narr: That's right, the nets were full of fish! And their friends came to help bring them in. Afterwards, Simon went to Jesus and said. . .

B: Wow! You can come fishing with us any

day. . .

Narr: No, actually he fell on his knees before Jesus and said, 'Go away from me, Lord, I am a sinful man!'

A: Wow! He realized just how amazing Jesus was!

Narr: Yes. Jesus said to Simon and his friends, 'Don't be afraid; from now on you will be catching people.' So they pulled the boats up on the beach, left everything and followed Jesus.

B: What, everything?

Narr: Yep! Everything!

A: Even the fish they had just caught?

Narr: Yep, even the fish! They realized that Jesus was worth following. And their lives were totally changed when they chose to follow Jesus.

A and B: Wow! (*They turn their backs to audience and stand as before.*)

Quiz 2, memory verse recap, prayer and theme song

Starship Discovery

BLAST OFF

***TURNING**—Peter chooses to follow Jesus*

Can you help the Starship Discovery to find the right path?

*Complete today's memory verse —
and then see if you can memorise it.*

Choose _____ t____ ____ you ____ s____, as for __,

I ____ serve ___ L____.

Joshua 24 verse 15

Give Peter and his friends a splash of colour!

Think of a time when you had to make a choice.

Did you make a good choice or a bad choice?

How could your choice have been different?

What difference would it have made?

Write your answers or draw a picture in the space below.

Day 2

BEAM ME UP

Trusting; Peter walks on the water

Aim

To show what happens when we put our trust in Jesus. Peter puts his trust in Jesus and walks on the water. When he takes his eyes off Jesus and turns his attention to the world around him he begins to sink. But he soon discovers that Jesus will still hold him fast.

Warm up

See Day 1

Theme Song

See Day 1

Theme illustration

You'll need to choose a volunteer and two leaders. Ask the volunteer if they trust you and then proceed to test their trust. Tell the volunteer that you are going to blindfold them and then ask them to fall backwards and be caught. (To increase the tension and make this more visual you can stand the volunteer on a chair for them to fall off backwards—providing their size and your strength match up!) Congratulate them on their trust, then say you want to try it one more time. As you are explaining this, walk round to the front of the volunteer so that, when you talk to them, they are disorientated as to your whereabouts. Meanwhile, your second leader should silently position themselves behind the volunteer. You then ask the volunteer to fall backwards again and be caught. (The second leader of course, unbeknown to them, will be the catcher this time). They may or may not conform—this doesn't really matter. Ask them how they felt the second time. You can point out how trustworthy they were if they did do it. If they didn't, it just reinforces the fact that it is hard to trust when we feel we are not in control!

Drama/Adventure story

The final frontier: II

Computer: Space. . . it's really big out there. This is the computer's log of the Starship Discovery, star date. . . We are continuing our mission, to explore the distant reaches of the universe and to seek out a planet as yet undiscovered by Annie Kerr-Ice. The computers on board ship have scanned a planet known as Earth to find a crew suitable for such a mission. All data received has been input and analysed. A suitable crew was found, but unfortunately they were busy, so we got. . . The Watt Family!

(*Enter Grandma, Rick and Wendy. They take up positions as at the end of previous day's drama*). Mummy Watt is trapped aboard the Tarragon ship, having been accidentally teleported by Wendy.

Wendy: I thought it was the TV.

Rick: I never did get to see the next thrilling installment of. . . (*current TV programme*).

Grandma: How will she ever escape?

Rick: Who? (*names TV character*)

Grandma: No, Mummy Watt, you 'narna!

Wendy: Will we ever see her again?

Rick: Who will do the cleaning?

Grandma: Who will keep Rick and Wendy out of trouble?

Rick and Wendy: Who will keep Grandma under control?

Computer: But most important of all—who will cook the dinner?

Rick: I'm starving!

Grandma: Well, I'm going to put my feet up and have a nice cup of tea.

Rick: Well, in that case, I might just as well play video games all day, I've got no one to nag me now, so I might as well enjoy being able to live in a mess.

Wendy: I can't believe you two! You're so selfish! We need to think of a plan to rescue Mum. Rick, have you seen the phone book? Let's look up the Tarragon's number and telephone them.

Rick: Don't be daft, Wendy! Your mobile phone's not going to work out here! This is the distant reaches of the universe not. . . (*Mention local landmark*).

Wendy: Oh, what a fool I am! But there must be something we can do!

Computer: Ahem. . .

Wendy: Oh! Do you think the computer could link up with them?

Rick: Well, we could give it a try. (*They crowd round the computer screen*)

Grandma: Here we are, here's a list of Tarragon's using the Internet.

Wendy: Chicken Tarragon. . .

Rick: Herbert Tarragon. . .

Grandma: Tarragon sauce. . .

Wendy: Tarragon soup. . .

Rick: I'm starving!

Wendy: Here we are! Enemy ship Tarragon!

Grandma: Patch them through the computer, Rick.

Computer: They aren't going to give you Mummy Watt back. She's too good at doing their ironing and their ship looks cleaner than it's ever looked before.

Wendy: Can't you bargain with them?

Computer: I've tried talking to their computer, but it drives a really hard bargain.

Wendy: Well, we've got to think of something!

Computer: I'm thinking! (*Whirring noises etc.*)

Rick: Come on, computer, get it together—I'm starving!

Computer: I've come up with a solution. . .

All three: Yes?

Computer: The Tarragons would be happy to swap Mummy Watt for someone who's wiser and has more experience.

Grandma: That's a jolly good idea! Who could that be?

Rick and Wendy: Not me! (*They look at Grandma*) So that leaves just one person!

Grandma: (*Realizing they mean her*) Eh, well, perhaps it's not such a good idea after all!

Computer: My ideas are always brilliant!

Grandma: Well, I'd give this idea the boot!

Computer: Trust me, I know what I'm doing. Gather round and I'll tell you my plan! (*They gather round the computer screen*)

Wendy: Oh!

Rick: Do you think it would work?

Grandma: Celery soup?

Rick: I'm starving!

Wendy: No, Gran, not celery soup! Substitute!

Grandma: What!

Computer: Trust me! Off you go and do as I say. (*All three leave stage. They return with a mop dressed up to look like Grandma*)

Grandma: I must remember to book a hair appointment when we get back home.

Wendy: Come on, put it in the teleport—and stand clear.

Rick: Here we go! (*He presses teleport switch*)

Mummy Watt: (*Appears in teleport as mop disappears*) And if you don't tidy that up I'll turn you into tarragon jelly! Oh! Hello! Rick, have you tidied your room yet? And get your feet off the table!

Wendy: Mummy! You're safe!

Rick: I'm starving! What's for lunch!

Computer: Red alert! Red alert! (*Klaxon sounds*) The Tarragons are not pleased with the substitution!

Grandma: I knew I should have got my hair done!

Computer: Red alert! Red alert! The Tarragons are attacking!

Mummy Watt: I knew I should have turned them into jelly!

Computer: Red alert! Red alert! The Tarragons have surrounded the ship! (*All freeze. To audience*) Is there any way out for the crew? Will the Tarragons blow them to smithereens? Will Grandma ever understand what's going on? Will Rick and Wendy ever be able to make their own packed lunches? Will Mummy Watt ever be able to get the spaceship shipshape again? YOU'LL HAVE TO WAIT UNTIL TOMORROW TO FIND OUT WHAT HAPPENS. . .

Drama/Adventure story link

Phew! What a sticky one that was! The Watt crew had to trust the computer when it came to getting their Mum back. They weren't sure at first, but they decided to trust the computer's plan. Trust is a strange thing. It usually means doing something we're not too sure of, but going ahead with it anyway. Jesus wants us to trust him. Sometimes that means that we need to do things that, deep down, we know are right, but we don't necessarily understand them at the time.

Memory verse

Proverbs 3:5 'Trust in the Lord with all your heart and lean not on your own understanding.'

A song: The sheet music can be found in Appendix B on page 146. The song can be found on the *Ultimate Holiday Club Guide* cassette, available from your local Christian bookshop, or, in case of difficulty, direct from BRF.

Quiz

Questions could include:

What never asks questions, but gets plenty of answers?
A doorbell

What goes up and down but never moves?
A staircase

What gets lost every time you stand up?
Your lap

What is always coming but never arrives?
Tomorrow

Puppets

Bert: Lucy, Lucy, how do you fancy coming for a swim later on?

Lucy: Er. . . well. . . er. . .

Bert: Go on, it'll be ace.

Lucy: Er. . . No, thanks.

Bert: Oh go on, Lucy, it's more fun with two.

Lucy: I can't.

Bert: Why not?

Lucy: I've got to er. . . um. . . walk the budgie!

Bert: Walk the budgie?

Lucy: No, er. . . hoover the lawn!

Bert: Lucy, you're making excuses. Come on, say 'yes!'

Lucy: No!

Bert: Why?

Lucy: 'Cos I don't want to!

Bert: Why not?

Lucy: 'Cos I don't!

Bert: But why Lucy?

Lucy: Because I can't swim—OK?

Bert: You can't swim?

Lucy: No!

Bert: Well, why didn't you say so?

Lucy: I thought you'd all laugh at me.

Bert: Don't be silly—we all didn't swim once. Look, why don't I teach you?

Lucy: What now?

Bert: Well, not all of it. But I can tell you what you have to do.

Lucy: Oh, I'm not sure. . .

Bert: I'm sorry, I forgot to ask—would you like to learn?

Lucy: Yes. Yes I would.

Bert: And you do trust me?

Lucy: Of course I do.

Bert: OK. Well, first you need a swimming costume.

Lucy: Yep! Got one of those!

Bert: Then when you get in the water. . .

Lucy: . . . In the water! Yuck! I'd get all wet!

Bert: Of course you would, silly. You can't swim otherwise!

Lucy: Oh! OK, what's next?

Bert: Well, you need to be able to hold your breath.

Lucy: What, like this? (*She takes a deep breath*)

Bert: Yeah, that's good. Then you sort of kick your legs and move your arms and. . . (*Lucy begins to wobble*). . . Lucy, are you all right?

Lucy: Mmm. Mmm.

Bert: OK, OK, let it out!

Lucy: Phew! How was that? (*Breathless*)

Bert: Very good—I think the rest we'll have to do in the pool.

Lucy: Oh yeah! I'm all excited now—can we go?

Bert: Well, I suppose so.

Lucy: Come on, Bert! I want to learn! Bye everyone.

Bert: Good grief, she's gone! I'd better make sure she's all right! Bye everyone.

Bible story

Peter walks on the water. Read the account in Matthew 14:22–32.

Key points

● *Peter's attempt to copy Jesus is a vivid lesson about the role of faith in following Jesus.*

● *We can easily identify with Peter's impulsive, yet vulnerable, personality.*

● *Peter doesn't attempt to do what is naturally impossible until he hears the command from Jesus.*

● *Peter is obedient to Jesus' call.*

● *Peter loses faith when he allows fear to get in the way.*

● *Peter turns to Jesus for help when he feels his faith failing.*

Style suggestion

Cast: Narrator and two others (A and B)

Narr: Have you ever been with your friends and had a mega-exciting day. On the way home you just have to talk about it!

A: Wow! What a day!

B: Excellent!

Narr: I'm sure this happened a lot in the Bible—especially if you hung around with Jesus.

A: One day had been a particularly long but

exciting day. . .

B: Jesus told the disciples to get into the boat and meet him across the other side of the lake.

Narr: He went off up a mountain to pray. While he was gone you can just imagine the sort of conversation they may have had!

A: Wow! What a day!

B: Excellent!

A: All those people!

B: Must have been thousands!

A: Thousands! At least five thousand men, plus all the women and kids!

B: And nothing for lunch!

A: Except what that little lad had—five loaves and two small pickled fish!

B: What a miracle! I couldn't believe my eyes. Five loaves, two fish, plus Jesus. . .

A: . . . and we all had plenty to eat.

Narr: Remember they were on the boat—chatting away. Tired after the long, hot day and now far out on the lake. The boat began to be tossed about by a rising wind. When suddenly. . .

A: Aaagh! Can you see what I see??

B: W. . . w. . . what?

A: There's someone walking towards us!

B: Walking! On the water!? Don't be daft! (*Turns to look*) Aaagh! There *is* someone walking on the water!

A and B: (*Both scream*) IT'S A GHOST!!

Narr: Hang on a minute you two. Look closer.

B: It's Jesus!

Narr: It was Jesus, walking on the water towards them. He said. . .

A: Courage, it is I. Don't be afraid!

B: Lord, if it is really you, order me to come out on the water to you.

A: Come!

Narr: So Peter got out of the boat and started walking on the water towards Jesus.

(*B mimes stepping out of the boat and walking carefully in slow motion.*)

Narr: Suddenly he noticed the strong wind. He became frightened and started to sink.

B: Save me, Lord!

Narr: Jesus reached out his hand and grabbed hold of him. 'What little faith you have! Why did you doubt?' said Jesus as they both climbed into the boat.

A and B: Truly you are the Son of God!

A: Ha! Fancy Peter failing like that! He must have known that Jesus would save him!

Narr: Yes, but at least he was prepared to have a go. He was willing to trust Jesus and put his faith in him.

B: Yes, the other disciples just watched. It was Peter who stepped out in faith.

Narr: You're right. Peter might have started to sink, but he was able to experience for himself how firmly Jesus was holding on to him.

A: I suppose the others missed out.

Narr: So be like Peter—put your trust in Jesus.

A: You may get scared and fail from time to time. . .

B: But Jesus will always be with you.

Quiz 2, memory verse recap, prayer and theme song

Starship Discovery

TRUSTING—*Peter walks on the water*

Starting in the arrow at the top of the spaceman's head, can you find your way to his heart?

You'll find the story of Peter walking on the water in Matthew's Gospel, chapter 14, verses 22 to 33. Read the story and then find all these words from the story in the wordsearch.

disciples Jesus boat evening ghost
waves Peter wind walked sink
save hand doubt worshipped

```
t a o b t r d e k l a w
b e s t w J i v n t u e
u l o i r e d a w i t d
o h n a l s l s y o e u
d d r h e u a r t p a n
d n l d i s c i p l e s
e a a n n o t i o n v y
o h u r g o h w n u e n
d e r h s s t a s i n k
n d o i r n g p r o i u
e s r o b s c w h a n p
t t w e r t u a r e g e
w e t v e r s v e f t v
r f s e m e r e t e P m
s o r o r y v s e r s e
```

 *Colour in today's memory verse.*

Trust in the Lord with all your heart and lean not on your own understanding

Try to imagine what it would be like to be Peter.
How do you think you would feel? _____
Would you trust Jesus as much as Peter did?_____
Who do you trust most? _____
Who do you think trusts you most? _____
What does it mean to trust in God?_____

Write your answers on the lines or draw a picture in the space below.

Day 3

BLACK HOLE

Tripping; Peter's denial and the message of the cross

Aim

To show that we all make mistakes. In fact, it's because we do things wrong and need help that Jesus came and died for us.

Warm up

See Day 1

Theme song

See Day 1

Theme illustration

This is a simple and effective illustration that reinforces the true meaning of what Jesus did on the cross, relating it to how we use crosses in our every day lives. Cross number one is something that every child will be familiar with at some point in their school life. When we do something wrong the teacher points it out with a cross, therefore a cross means 'wrong'. Cross number two might make them giggle with embarrassment, because these are the sort that you find at the bottom of a valentine's card. They stand for kisses, and so a cross also means 'love'. Cross number three you may not

discover until you are eligible to vote. You place a cross on a voting slip to indicate your preference, therefore a cross means 'choice'. This is exactly what the cross of Jesus points to as well. Jesus died on the cross because of the wrong things that we have done. He did not have to, but he went to the cross because of his love for us. When we accept this and believe it in our hearts then we have made a choice to follow him.

Drama/Adventure story

The final frontier: III

Computer: Space. . . it's bigger than we thought. This is the computer's log of the Starship Discovery, star date. . . We are continuing our mission, to explore the distant reaches of the universe and to seek out a planet as yet undiscovered by Neil Strongarm. The computers onboard ship have done a deal with the computers on the enemy ship Tarragon in a bid to rescue Mummy Watt. The rescue worked but the plans went awry when the Tarragons discovered that Grandma was a mop! (*Enter Grandma, Mummy, Rick and Wendy. They take up positions as at the end of previous day's drama*).

Grandma: Hey! Who are you calling a mop?

Computer: Red alert! Red alert!

Mummy: Oh, don't start that again, I've got a headache!

Computer: The Tarragons are chasing us. Quick, Rick, get behind the gear stick.

Wendy: Now, let's be sensible. Let's look at the map. Which way, Grandma?

Grandma: Left a bit, right a bit. Up. Down. In. Out. Put your right foot in, put your right foot out. You do the Hokey Cokey and you turn about. . .

Mummy: Get on with it, Grandma, stop messing about.

Rick: Look there's a black hole over there, we can hide in that!

Computer: No, no! Stay away! Steer round it! Go the other way!

Rick: Too late! We're getting sucked in!

Grandma: Aaaahh! My teesh are coming loosh!

Wendy: Hold on tight, Grandma!

Computer: (*Speech slowing down*) We're getting sucked in. I'm—fading—away. Head—for—the—centre.

Grandma: Watsh out for meteoritesh! (*Crew are bumped around*) Shteer left, Rick (*Her speech is slowing down*) Shteer—right—Rick. (*Crew move around in slow motion and finally everything comes to a halt*)

Wendy: (*Dazed and with slow speech*) Where—are—we,—Grandma?

Grandma: How—should—I—know? Thish—ishn't— on—my— map,—it'sh—jusht—a—big,—black—hole.

Mummy: Let's—ask—the—computer. (*They gather round the computer screen, but there is no response*)

Rick: Maybe—he's—asleep.

Wendy: Don't—be—stupid,—computers—don't—sleep.

Grandma: He'sh—malfunctioned.

Rick: What—does—that—mean?

Wendy: It—means—it's—broken,—stupid. (*Sad music and audience response*)

Grandma: (*Sobbing*) He—wash—shuch—a—good—old— chip—I—mean—chap. It—wash—a—brilliant—reshcue—plan. Who—elshe—would—have—thought—of—it?

Wendy: Who—else—would—have—chosen—us—to—help—explore—the—far reaches—of—outer—space?

Mummy: He—thought—we—were—very—special. He—even—let—me—clean—his—screen. (*She rubs the computer screen with her duster*)

Computer: (*Whirring noises*) Thank you very much! That feels a lot better.

Mummy: (*Speech returns to normal*) What did you say, Rick!

Rick: I didn't say anything! I think it was the computer!

Wendy: Oh, you're so thick, Rick! Anyone can see that the computer has died!

Grandma: (*Gulps*) Ah, my teeth seem to have refitted themselves—that's better. Yes, I'll miss him so much. I loved being celery souped for a mop!

Computer: You're going to make me cry in a minute!

Mummy: You said that without moving your lips, Rick!

Rick: It wasn't me!

Computer: Booting up! Booting up!

All: He's alive! Hooray!

Computer: We are coming out of the black hole. Your driving must have been really slick, Rick!

Rick: The only trouble is, I've no idea where we are!

Wendy: We're safely through—but lost!

Grandma: Where's my knitting?

Mummy: Will Rick's hair ever be tidy again?

Computer: Will my memory ever be the same again?

Mummy: Will Wendy ever be able to use her mobile phone?

Computer: What's for dinner? How will we ever get home? YOU'LL HAVE TO WAIT UNTIL TOMORROW TO FIND OUT. . .

Rick: I'm starving!

Drama/Adventure story link

Phew! That was a close one for the computer today. It seemed for a while that the Watt family had lost him as they went through the black hole. The family felt sad and a bit lost without him, but it wasn't the end. Soon he was back on line again. It was a bit of a mistake to drift into the black hole, but, you know, all of us make mistakes from time to time. We need to stop ourselves and put things right again, before we get into a bigger hole than we are already in! God knows what we are like, and he knows that we need his help. That's why Jesus came to live on earth and do the things he did—even being willing to die—because of the mistakes we make. We shouldn't make the mistake of forgetting to say 'sorry', and then 'thank you' for what Jesus has done for us.

Memory verse

1 Timothy 1:15: 'Christ Jesus came into the world to save sinners.'

A song: The sheet music can be found in Appendix B on page 146. The song can be found on the *Ultimate Holiday Club Guide* cassette, available from your local Christian bookshop, or, in case of difficulty, direct from BRF.

Quiz

Questions could include:

Who was the fastest runner in history?
Adam—he was first in the human race!

Which vegetable is the fastest?
The runner bean!

What did Lucy want to learn to do yesterday?
Swim.

What did Bert say she had to do?
Trust him.

Puppets

Lucy: Bert! Bert! Have you seen my painting?

Bert: Oh, hello, Lucy! Have I seen your what?

Lucy: My painting. I've lost my painting.

Bert: What was it of?

Lucy: It was of the Starship discovery.

Bert: Oh, was it sort of silvery and black?

Lucy: Yes, that's right. Have you seen it, Bert?

Bert: Sort of. Erm. . . I didn't realize that's what it was.

Lucy: Well, where is it?

Bert: I was a bit bored, so I used it to make a paper aeroplane.

Lucy: You did what! A paper aeroplane!

Bert: Yes, I'm sorry, Lucy. I just didn't realize it was yours.

Lucy: But that took me hours—well, minutes, anyway.

Bert: Yeah, but it was only a picture.

Lucy: No, Bert, it was *my* picture—not *yours*—and *I* wanted to bring it today to show everyone.

Bert: I'm sorry, Lucy. It was wrong of me, I know.

Lucy: Well, what am I going to do now? I've got nothing to show everyone.

Bert: Will you forgive me, Lucy?

Lucy: Erm. . .

Bert: Please?

Lucy: Well, yes, I suppose so. But what am I going to do?

Bert: How about I give you a hand to do a new picture?

Lucy: Hey, that's a good idea! We could make a really big one, with bottle tops and everything stuck on it!

Bert: What, like the frieze that everyone is making at holiday club?

Lucy: Yeah! Brill!

Bert: Come on then, Lucy. Say goodbye.

Lucy: Bye, everyone!

Bert: Bye!

Bible story

Peter denies Jesus. Read the four accounts in Matthew 26:69–75, Mark 14:66–72, Luke 22:56–62 and John 18:15–18 and 25–27.

Key Points

● *Peter's denial stands in sharp contrast to Jesus' bold confession before the council.*

● *Peter digs himself deeper and deeper into his sin with each successive challenge about his identity.*

● *We are more liable to fail Jesus in the heat of the moment, or the depth of our despair.*

● *Jesus understands our humanity.*

● *Jesus meets us in our remorse.*

Style suggestion

Cast: Narrator and two others (A and B)

Narr: It's easy to say one thing and then do another.

A: I did that once. Mum and Dad were going out and I said I would do *all* the washing up and cleaning!

B: Wow! You said THAT!

A: Yep!

Narr: Did you?

A: Did I what?

Narr: Do all the washing up and cleaning?

A: Er. . . No! I. . . er. . . forgot. I meant to, though!

Narr: That sort of thing happens a lot—when someone says that they'll do something and they really, really. . .

B: Really, really, really, really. . .

Narr: . . . mean it. But in the end they don't do it—for many different reasons.

A: Peter thought Jesus was great!

B: The greatest!

Narr: He knew Jesus was more than just a man.

A: He had realized that Jesus was the Son of God.

B: He thought that Jesus was great!

A: The greatest!

Narr: But Peter knew there was trouble ahead.

A: He knew lots of people wanted Jesus out of the way.

B: They were jealous because Jesus was so popular.

Narr: But Peter had decided *he* would protect Jesus.

A: He would *die* for him if he had to!

B: I will never leave you, even though all the rest do!

Narr: I tell you that before the cock crows twice tonight, you will say three times that you do not know me.

B: I will never say that, even if I have to die with you!

A: And he meant it. He really meant it!

Narr: Soon after that, while Jesus was praying in the Garden of Gethsemane a crowd armed with swords and clubs came to arrest Jesus.

B: Peter drew his sword and swung it viciously at the crowd.

A: But he was a fisherman, not a soldier.

B: He struck at the High Priest's slave, cutting off his ear.

A: Jesus touched the slave's ear and healed him and said. . .

Narr: Did you have to come with swords and clubs to capture me, as though I were an outlaw?

A: Then they arrested Jesus and all the disciples left him and ran away.

B: But Peter followed them from a distance and went into the courtyard of the high priest's house. He joined those who were sitting round the courtyard fire. A servant girl came up to him and said. . .

A: You, too, were with Jesus of Galilee.

B: I don't know what you're talking about!

Narr: Then another servant girl saw him. . .

A: He was with Jesus of Nazareth!

B: I swear I don't know that man!

Narr: After a little while the men standing there came to Peter. One of them said. . .

A: Of course you are one of them. After all, the way you speak gives you away!

B: I swear that I am telling the truth! May God punish me if I am not! I do not know that man!

Narr: Just then a cock crowed, and Peter remembered what Jesus had told him. . .

A: Before the cock crows, you will say three times that you do not know me.

Narr: Peter went out and wept bitterly.

B: I've let Jesus down. My best mate!

A: I reckon if a crowd had accused him, he would have stood up for Jesus. He'd have been prepared to fight for him.

B: But it was a servant girl. I wasn't prepared for that. I panicked. . . and failed.

A: He must have felt really awful.

B: Why did Jesus choose me? I told him I was useless—but he still chose me.

Narr: God loves to choose weak people. People who know they just can't do things on their own. People who realize they need God's help.

A: Later on, Jesus forgave Peter.

B: And Peter went on to speak up for Jesus.

Narr: God knows we will all make mistakes, but he longs to forgive us.

A and B: Because God really does love us!
(*Thumbs up*)

Quiz 2, memory verse recap, prayer and theme song

Starship Discovery

TRIPPING—Peter denies Jesus

Draw a picture of Starship Discovery being sucked towards the Black Hole.

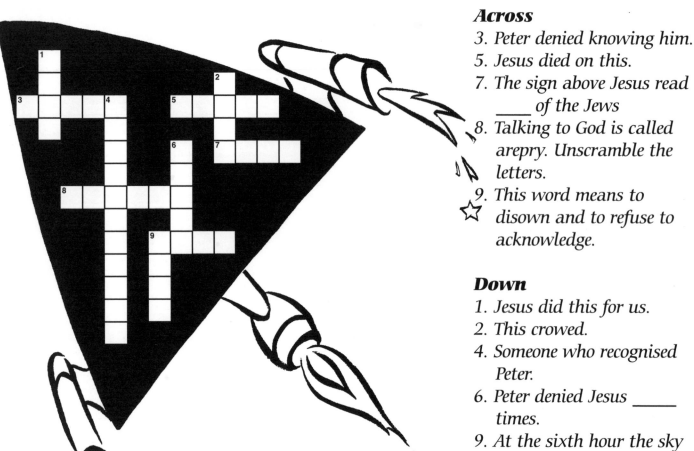

Across

3. Peter denied knowing him.
5. Jesus died on this.
7. The sign above Jesus read ____ of the Jews
8. Talking to God is called arepry. Unscramble the letters.
9. This word means to disown and to refuse to acknowledge.

Down

1. Jesus did this for us.
2. This crowed.
4. Someone who recognised Peter.
6. Peter denied Jesus ____ times.
9. At the sixth hour the sky went ____.

Rearrange the words to find today's memory verse.

into came the save Christ sinners to world Jesus

_____ ____ ____ ___ _____ __ ____ _____.

1 Timothy 1 verse 15

When we are frightened we can talk to God.
Write your prayer here.

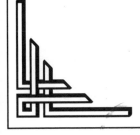

Day 4

BREAKTHROUGH

Transforming; Peter is transformed

Aim

To show that just as Peter and the disciples were transformed when the Holy Spirit came at Pentecost, so we, when we receive him, begin a life-changing transformation process.

Warm up

See Day 1

Theme song

See Day 1

Theme illustration

For this you will need a Polaroid camera with no film in it. Talk about the merits of photography and say what wonderful photographs you are going to take of everyone. Pretend to take lots of pictures with the camera, then make the discovery that it hasn't got a film in it. Look disappointed. Prime a leader to come on stage at this point with a film—gift wrapped. Load the camera, then take a photograph. Proudly show the audience the photo, then explain that actually the camera was not really doing what it should do the first time you tried to take pictures with it, because it was missing the one crucial requirement—a film. The camera was only able to fulfil its function once it had a film in it—the end result being—a photograph. Explain that we are like the camera. When God gives us his Holy Spirit, he changes our lives and helps us to be the people he meant us to be. Just like the camera was meant to have a film to work properly, so God wants us to have the gift of his Holy Spirit in order to live life to the full.

Drama/Adventure story

The final frontier: IV

Computer: Space. . . it's really big out there. This is the computer's log of the Starship Discovery, star date. . . We are continuing our mission, to explore the distant reaches of the universe and to seek out a planet as yet undiscovered by Cynic the Hogdeheg. We had a bit of a bumpy ride when we were sucked into a black hole. For a while everyone had to manage without me. But I sparked back to life and to everyone's relief we have come through and are back on course. . . or are we?? (*Enter Grandma, Mummy, Rick and Wendy. They take up positions as at end of previous day's drama.*)

Wendy: Where are we?

Grandma: How should I know? We've gone right off the map.

Mummy: Perhaps the computer knows.

Computer: Searching records. Searching records. (*Whirring noises*)

Mummy: Come on, computer dear, you can do it!

Computer: It's no good. Some of my files were damaged when I crashed. I can't find the right path.

Rick: Can you help him everyone? Do you know where we are? (*Audience responds*)

Grandma: What did they say? The back of beyond?

Wendy: I think they must have said the middle of nowhere.

Mummy: We'll never get it ironed out at this rate. I think I'll go and make a nice cup of tea.

Computer: Red alert! Red alert! The Tarragons have followed us through the black hole. Battlestations! Battlestations! Shields up! Missiles ready!

Grandma: Miss Isle? Who's she? I've never heard of her!

Computer: There's a message coming through from the Tarragons' computer. (*They all crowd round the computer screen*)

Rick: (*Reading*) DON'T SHOOT!

Wendy: It's a trick!

Rick: (*Reading*) THIS IS NOT A TRICK. WE ARE SORRY WE TRIED TO KEEP YOUR MUMMY HOSTAGE.

Mummy: Ah, that's nice. Is that you, Herbert?

Rick: (*Reading*) YES, IT'S ME, MUMMY WATT. WE ARE LOST. CAN YOU HELP US?

Grandma: Herbert? Who's Herbert?

Mummy: That's Herbert Tarragon—Herb for short.

Wendy: Can they be trusted?

Rick: (*Reading*) THANK YOU FOR LENDING US YOUR GRANDMA, SHE WAS VERY USEFUL.

Grandma: Oh, thank you very much!

Rick: (*Reading*) LET'S HELP EACH OTHER TO FIND OUR WAY BACK HOME. WE WILL BEAM YOUR GRANDMA BACK.

Wendy: But can we trust them?

Mummy: Well, they didn't shoot. . .

Grandma: And here's the mop! (*Mop appears in teleport*)

Computer: There is no way we can get back home with just our power. The best thing to do is to link the two spaceships together and navigate with a tractor beam.

Rick: (*Reading*) AGREED. They agree!

Computer: Tarragon ship docking! Tarragon ship docking!

Mummy: They're giving us the extra boost we need!

Wendy: Steer us round the black hole, Rick!

Rick: Hold on tight! (*Crew hold on as the ship gathers speed*)

Computer: Tarragon forces ahead!

Rick: (*Reading*) THANK YOU. WE ARE LEAVING YOU NOW AND RE-UNITING WITH OUR OWN FLEET.

Grandma: We're back on the map! Look, here's the way home.

Wendy: (*Answering mobile phone*) Hello? Yes, this is Wendy Watt. Oh, hello, Herbert? Oh, do you think so? Oh, that's nice? Well, if you say so. . .

Computer: Could this be the start of a wonderful relationship with the Tarragons? Will Wendy ever get off the phone to her Tarragon friend? Will Grandma's teeth ever be the same after having been sucked through the black hole? Will Rick ever grow up? Will Mummy ever make that cup of tea? Have the Watt family finally discovered the final frontier? Will they all live happily ever after?

All: Will you shut down!

Drama/Adventure story link

What an adventure! What a transformation too! The Tarragons hadn't seemed very friendly to start off with, but they ended up realizing that they were just as stuck as the Watt family. What a difference it made when they worked together! Jesus transforms our lives when we allow his Holy Spirit to help us. He promises never to leave us and, when we let him, he can do great things through us—especially when we work together.

Memory verse

Joshua 1:5 'I will always be with you; I will never abandon you.'

A song: The sheet music can be found in Appendix B on page 146. The song can be found on the *Ultimate Holiday Club Guide* cassette, available from your local Christian bookshop, or, in case of difficulty, direct from BRF.

Quiz

Questions could include:

When is a car not a car?
When it turns into a garage.

What has one horn and gives milk?
A milk float.

Which Tarragon did Wendy take a liking to?
Herbert.

Who nearly had her teeth sucked through the black hole?
Grandma Watt.

Puppets

Bert: Lucy! Lucy!

(*Lucy snores—out of sight*)

Bert: Can you help me, everyone? I think Lucy is asleep!

(*Lucy snores loudly*)

Bert: Yup! I'll count to three and then we'll all shout 'Wake up, Lucy!' Are you ready? 1—2—3 !

All: WAKE UP, LUCY!

Lucy: Aaaaaaaaghhh!

Bert: What a racket, Lucy! What was all that about?

Lucy: Oh, Bert, it was horrible!

Bert: What was?

Lucy: My dream. I had a horrible dream.

Bert: What, like a nightmare?

Lucy: Yes, that's right.

Bert: Well, why don't you tell us about it? Maybe we can help to make you feel better.

Lucy: Are you sure?

Bert: Well, we can try.

Lucy: OK—it all started with my paper round...

Bert: You're right, that is scary!

Lucy: Why do I get the feeling you're not taking this very seriously?

Bert: I'm sorry, Lucy—go on.

Lucy: Well, I got halfway round and then I came to number 37—you know, that big old house. . .

Bert: Oh yes, I know, the tumble-down one on the hill.

Lucy: That's right. Well, I got there and I was just about to put the paper through the letter-box when I heard this woof, woof, woof.

Bert: What, you mean a cat?

Lucy: No silly!

Bert: Oh, you mean a budgie?

Lucy: No! It was their dog and, as I pushed the paper through the letter-box, he grabbed it and yanked it out of my hand. I thought he was going to jump through the letter-box and eat me!

Bert: Lucy, how big was this dog?

Lucy: Oh, huge! About the size of an elephant!

Bert: And how big was the letter-box?

Lucy: Well, normal size, of course. About the size of your mouth!

Bert: Thank you, Lucy! So a dog the size of an elephant was going to jump through a letter-box the size of my mouth?

Lucy: Yeah, well I was scared, OK? And I don't want to do my paper round now.

Bert: But, Lucy, you'll be all right!

Lucy: How do you know? I'm frightened!

Bert: How about if I came with you?

Lucy: Would you?

Bert: Of course, that's what friends are for.

Lucy: Oh, Bert, that would be much better! You promise you won't leave me?

Bert: No, I won't leave you.

Lucy: Even at number 37?

Bert: Especially then!

Lucy: Oh, thank you, Bert! Come on and help me to get ready. Bye everyone!

Bert: OK, I'm coming! Bye!

Bible story

Pentecost. Read the account in Acts 2.

Key points

● *Jesus' promises always come true.*

● *Jesus will always help us speak boldly for him.*

● *Jesus turns our weakness into strength.*

Style suggestion

Cast: Narrator and two others (A and B)

Narr: Have you ever had a friend. . .

A: A best friend. . .

B: A friend who you do everything with, football, swimming, watching TV. . .

Narr: Then one day that friend says that they're moving.

A: (*To B*) Moving? Where?

B: Dad's got a new job, we've got to move!

A: You can't!

B: I've got to.

A: But. . . but. . . but—I don't want you to.

B: I don't want to either, but I've got to. (*Sad music; A and B hug emotionally and then move four steps apart, looking sad, blowing nose, wiping eyes, waving etc.*)

Narr: It's very sad when someone you love goes away.

A: You feel lonely. . .

B: What will you do without them?

Narr: That's what happened with Peter and the other disciples.

A: Jesus had died on the cross.

B: We felt lost without him.

Narr: But then he came back to life!

A and B: ALIVE! We're so happy!

Narr: But then he had to leave them again. . .

A and B: Oh, no!

Narr: But Jesus promised to send another, someone new. . .

A: Someone new?

B: No one could ever take Jesus' place.

Narr: Someone who would help them, someone who would give them strength. Someone who would guide them.

A and B: WHO??

Narr: The Holy Spirit. He is God, just as Jesus is God. He will always be with you. He will help you and give you strength. He will guide you and give you power.

A: Erm. . . you mean like a battery for a torch?

B: Don't be daft!

Narr: Well, yes, a bit like a battery for a torch. A torch is useless without the battery. It's the battery that provides the power and lights the torch!

A: But we feel so alone!

B: Who will protect us?

A: We really miss Jesus!

B: Yeah, we feel so weak and helpless. . .

A: And scared.

B: Yeah! Let's hide!

Narr: So they shut themselves away, all the disciples were together in one house.

A: Suddenly!

B: There was a noise from the sky!

A: It sounded like a strong wind blowing!

B: It filled the whole house!

A: Suddenly!

B: We saw what looked like tongues of fire!

A: Spreading out and touching each one of us!

Narr: And they were all filled with the Holy Spirit.

A: Suddenly!

B: We weren't scared any more!

A: We weren't weak any more!

Narr: The Holy Spirit, who Jesus had promised to send, had come!

A and B: Wow! We've got to tell everyone!

Narr: So they left the house and went into the street, and started to tell everyone about the great things God had done.

A: Everyone can understand us!

B: What, even those who can't speak the same language?

A: Yes, everyone can hear what we are saying in their own language!

Narr: It was a miracle. God's message was—in fact—*is* for everyone.

A: Everyone was amazed!

B: Confused!

Narr: As they heard the disciples telling them the good news, the people began to ask what they should do to follow Jesus.

A: Many people believed our message and were baptized.

B: Yeah, about 3,000.

Narr: Jesus hadn't abandoned them. His Holy Spirit was living inside them.

A and B: Thank you, Jesus!

Quiz 2, memory verse recap, prayer and theme song

Starship Discovery **BREAKTHROUGH**

***TRANSFORMING**—Peter is transformed*

At the space station you need to visit all the fuel ports once only. Can you find the way?

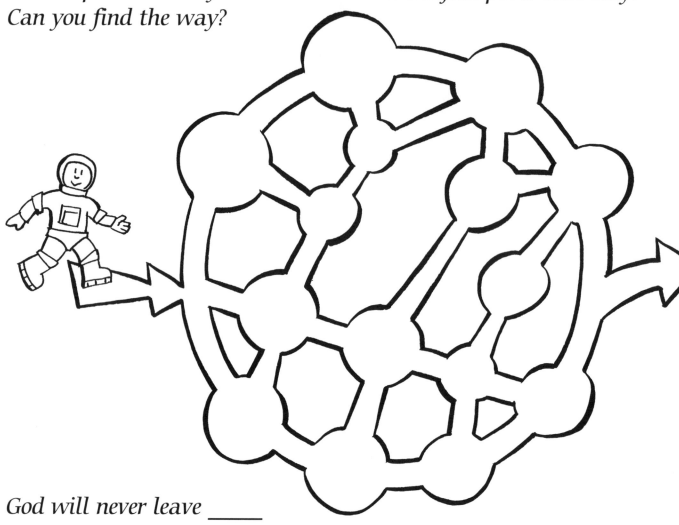

God will never leave _____

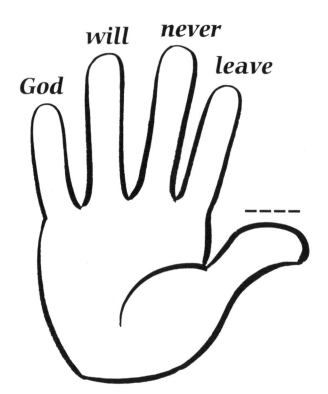

Put your name where the thumb is, then say this memory verse using your hand.

God   will   never   leave   _ _ _ _

Draw Peter and the disciples before the Holy Spirit came and then draw a picture of them after the Holy Spirit had come.

Before

After

Transform this picture by colouring in the o's to find out who God sent to stay with us.

Day 5

BATTLE STATIONS

Training; Peter's release from prison

Aim

To show that we need to be prepared for the journey ahead. It won't always be easy, but God is always with us and we have prayer as a powerful weapon.

Warm up

See Day 1

Theme song

See Day 1

Theme illustration

You will need a re-lighting candle. Light it and explain how God brings light to our lives. Go on to say that there are many things in life, or even people, that will 'knock us back' in our life with God. Invite someone to come on to the stage to try and blow out the candle. But despite all those things, God is always there and his light will shine.

Drama/Adventure story

The final frontier: V

After the computer beamed aboard the Watt family, life became one big adventure. They had been chosen because they were each good at one particular thing and, when they worked together, the starship could function as it was meant to. It's wasn't long, though, before something went wrong and Mummy Watt was beamed aboard the enemy Tarragon ship by mistake when Wendy was trying to turn on the TV for Rick—I'm sure she was only trying to be helpful. The computer managed to strike a deal with the Tarragons to trade Mummy Watt for

someone wiser and more experienced. Well, that could only mean Grandma, couldn't it? Did you think that the mop celery soup—I mean, substitute—was a good idea? But what about the way the Tarragons chased them into the black hole—that must have been really scary! And poor Grandma nearly loshed—I mean lost—her teeth! So there they were, no map and stuck for ever on the wrong side of a black hole. Or were they? The Tarragon's change of heart meant that they could help each other to get back, didn't it? By joining forces, they were able to get back to safety—forming some interesting friendships on the way. I do hope Wendy doesn't run up too large a bill on her mobile phone! What an adventure it all was!

You know, the Christian life may not always seem so adventurous, but it can be very exciting. God sometimes chooses us to do things for him which we would never imagine ourselves doing without him. And often when we get into a mess, we have to trust God to help us sort it out. God longs for us to be his friends. He wants to transform our lives with his Holy Spirit. When we turn to him and learn to trust him, he will start to transform us so, even when we trip, we can still carry on training to be in his team.

Memory verse

2 Corinthians 4:8–9 'Sometimes we are troubled, but not crushed; sometimes we're in doubt, but never in despair. There are many enemies, but we always have a friend; although badly hurt at times we are not destroyed.'

A song: The sheet music can be found in Appendix B on page 146. The song can be found on the *Ultimate Holiday Club Guide* cassette, available from your local Christian bookshop, or, in case of difficulty, direct from BRF.

Quiz

Questions could include:

What job did Peter do?
He was a fisherman.

In which strange place did Peter and the disciples see Jesus?
Walking on the water.

How many times did Peter deny Jesus?
Three.

What did Jesus send that transformed Peter and the other disciples?
His Holy Spirit.

Puppets

Bert: Lucy! Lucy!

Lucy: Mmm? Mmm?

Bert: What's wrong?

Lucy: Mmm! Mmm!

Bert: You were making me some toffee?

Lucy: Mmm! Mmm!

Bert: . . . but it went wrong?

Lucy: Mmm! Mmm!

Bert: . . . you thought you should try some?

Lucy: Mmm! Mmm!

Bert: . . . but it was stickier than you thought?

Lucy: Mmm! Mmm!

Bert: . . . and now your mouth is stuck?

Lucy: Mmm! Mmm!

Bert: Ha, ha! What a funny thing!

Lucy: Mmm! Mmm!

Bert: Well, I'm sorry. I do have to say, though, it's quite a transformation! You're usually so noisy, Lucy! I've never known you so quiet!

Lucy: Mmm! Mmm!

Bert: . . . you don't think that's very kind?

Lucy: Mmm! Mmm!

Bert: . . . and you thought friends were supposed to help each other?

Lucy: Mmm! Mmm!

Bert: Well, of course, Lucy! I was just making the most of the peace and quiet! But of *course* I'll rescue you.

Lucy: Mmm! Mmm!

Bert: OK! OK! Calm down! Let's go and get you some water or something. Say goodbye, Lucy.

Lucy: Mmm! Mmm!

Bert: Oh, no, you can't, can you?

Lucy: Mmm! Mmm!

Bert: Never mind. Bye, bye everyone. Come on Lucy!

Lucy: Mmm! Mmm!

Bible Story

Peter's release from prison. Read the account in Acts 12:6–19

Key points

● *Jesus was beside Peter, even though Peter was not aware of the fact.*

● *Jesus rescues us in ways that are sometimes beyond our wildest dreams.*

● *Peter's rescue was backed by the prayers of the disciples.*

● *When we pray, we should pray with the expectation that God will answer!*

● *God answers our prayers for a purpose.*

Style suggestion

Cast: Narrator and two others (A and B)

Narr: (*To A*) Do you ever dream?

A: (Excitedly) Oh yes! Sometimes I have really nice dreams and I'm ever so disappointed when I wake up. I try to go back to sleep again!

Narr: (*To B*) Do you ever dream?

B: Sometimes, but I often don't like my dreams. They scare me. When I have a nightmare I'm relieved to wake up!

A: (*To Narrator*) Do you ever dream?

Narr: Oh, yes! But my dreams never seem to make sense! Sometimes I dream that my friends and I are chatting away to TV stars—but in the strangest of places!

A: Dreams can sometimes seem so real!

Narr: Once a strange thing happened to Peter. . .

A: It was so strange that he wasn't sure whether he was dreaming or whether it was real!

B: Horrid King Herod Agrippa had had James, the brother of John, arrested and put to death.

Narr: Now he had arrested Peter and thrown him into jail—intending to have him put to death too.

A: The people of the church were praying earnestly to God for him.

B: Peter was chained between two guards. . .

A: And there were more guards on duty at the prison gate.

B: There was no escape!

Narr: Peter was fast asleep. . .

A: Fast asleep! How could he sleep at a time like this!

B: Perhaps he trusted God. . . (*He sinks to the floor and pretends to sleep*).

Narr: Suddenly an angel of the Lord stood there, and a light shone in the cell. The angel shook Peter by the shoulder, woke him up and said. . .

A: (*Shaking B by the shoulders*) Hurry! Get up!

Narr: At once the chains fell off Peter's hands. .

A: Fasten your belt and put on your sandals. (*B mimes this*) Put your cloak on and come with me.

Narr: The angel led Peter out of the prison. Peter followed him, not sure whether he was dreaming or not.

B: Past the first guard. . .

A: Didn't they wake up?

Narr: No!

A: Didn't they see him, then?

Narr: Apparently not!

B: . . . past the second guard. . .

A: Tut! Tut! Not sleeping on duty, surely!

Narr: Well, they were highly trained soldiers, they wouldn't sleep on duty but. . .

B: . . . and out through the iron gate leading to the city.

Narr: Peter walked free, down the city street. Then the angel left him.

B: Wow! Now I know that it is really true! The Lord sent his angel to rescue me from Herod's power!

Narr: He went to the home of Mary, the mother of John Mark. Many people had gathered there and were praying.

B: Rat-a-tat-tat!

A: Who is it?

B: It's me, Peter!

A: Peter who?

B: Peter Peter!

A: Wow!

Narr: The servant girl, Rhoda, ran back to the others. She was so excited she forgot to open the door!

A: It's Peter!

B: Peter who?

A: Peter Peter!

B: Are you mad! Peter's in prison—it must be his angel!

Narr: Eventually, they opened the door, and there was Peter! They were amazed to see him!

A: How daft!

Narr: What?

A: Why were they so amazed that God had rescued Peter? Why wouldn't they believe it was him?

B: Yeah, they had been praying all night that God would rescue him—and when he did they didn't believe it!

Narr: God really does hear our prayers. And he always answers them.

A: Isn't it brilliant to know that God listens to us when we talk to him!

B: It certainly is!

Quiz 2, memory verse recap, prayer and theme song

Drama workshop/crafts display

You may wish to consider an alternative to the previous day's system of rotation. This could give you space to prepare material for a Family Service, hold a drama workshop, or a create special craft display.

Starship Discovery

TRAINING—*Peter is released from prison*

Colour in the picture of Peter in prison. Can you see the angel?

 Unscramble the letters to find today's memory verse.

*We are sometimes **burtodle**, but not **durches**, sometimes we're in **botud**, but never in **spreadi**. There are many **meesien**, but we always have a **rinfed**; although badly **thur** at times, we are not **seetroddy**.*

Help Peter to find his way out of prison.

Wordsearch

```
P e t e r t w i g
i R a c h s p x u
g h a n g e l t a
s o p y g i l a r
g d p a i u e n d
a a a r z n c g s
t w t p l i g h t
f v i e r h o a d
v i s i o n a n t
```

Peter
praying
Rhoda
angel
guards
cell
gate
light
vision

Appendix A
Which Resources?

The Bible Reading Fellowship,
Peter's Way,
Sandy Lane West,
Oxford,
OX4 5HG
01865 748227

details of the cassette accompanying this
book are on page 160

Children Worldwide,
Dalesdown,
Honeybridge Lane,
Dial Post,
Horsham,
W Sussex
RH3 8MX
01403 710712

**Christian Publicity
Organization (CPO),**
Garcia Estate,
Canterbury Road,
Worthing,
W Sussex
BN13 1BW
01903 26456

**Church Pastoral Aid
Society (CPAS),**
Athena Drive,
Tachbrook Park,
Warwick
CV34 6BR
01926 334242

CWR,
Waverley Abbey House,
Waverley Lane,
Farnham,
Surrey
GU9 8EP
01252 783695

The Dynamite Club,
94 Kelvin Road,
Cubbington,
Leamington Spa,
Warwickshire
CV32 7TQ

ICC,
4 Regency Mews
Silverdale Road,
Eastbourne,
East Sussex
BN23 6NW
01323 643341

John Hardwick,
47 Whitestone Road,
Halesowen,
West Midlands
B63 3PU
0121 550 5794

**Juggling Junction,
(juggling equipment)**
Units 4/5 Polly Brooks Yard,
216, High Street,
Lye,
West Midlands,
DY9 8JX
01384 897474

Saltmine Trust,
PO Box 15,
Dudley,
W Midlands
DY3 2AN
01902 881080

Scripture Union,
207-209 Queensway,
Bletchley,
Milton Keynes,
Buckinghamshire,
MK2 2EB
01908 856000

Appendix B
Sheet Music

Theme 1
Theme song: The Adventure Cruise

Words + music by John Hardwick

We're go-ing on an adven-ture, on an adven-ture the Ad-venture Cruise — Come a join

— us on the adven-ture, on the adven-ture the Adventure Cruise —

1. Al —
2. The tho' we're going to have loads of fun We know the ocean is wide, But with Je-sus as our captain we know we've got the best guide Yes we're (2) wind may blow, (blow) the rain may fall, The lightning may flash, and the thunder may roar, We may get scared, (scream) Cos what can we do? But with Je-sus as our cap-tain we know we're gonna get through; Yes we're the Adven-ture Cruise.

Action Song: Choosing Song

Words & music by John Hardwick

Verse 2:
We choose a job we like a lot,
We choose to get married or maybe not,
Choose to ski in the cold or bathe in the hot,
Our lives are full of decisions.

I will never turn away

Words & music by John Hardwick

Verse 2:
I will never turn away
anyone who comes to me.

Everyone who calls

Words & music by John Hardwick

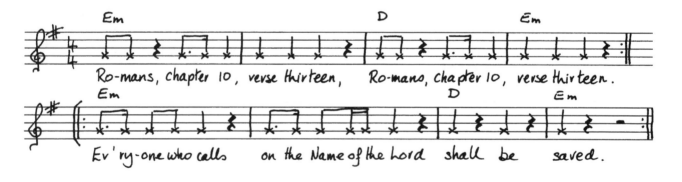

New Creation

Words & music by John Hardwick

When an-y-one (when an-y-one) Is joined to Christ (Is joined to Christ) He is a new (He is a new) crea — tion (crea — tion), The old has gone (the old has gone) The new has come (the new has come) He is a new (he is a new) crea — tion (crea — tion). Cor-inth — i — ans chapter 5 — verse se — ven-teen 2. Cor-inth — i — ans chapter 5 — verse se — ven — teen.

All who love God

Words & music by John Hardwick

In the first book of John chap-ter 4 — verse twenty-one, Christ gives us a command, that needs to be done —. All who L.O.V.E. G.O.D. Must al — so L.O.V.E. their bro-ther and their sis-ter —.

If anyone wants to come with me

Words & music by John Hardwick

Je-sus said in Matthew sixteen verse twenty four, Jesus said in Matthew sixteen verse twenty four: If an-y-one wants to come with me If

He must for-get him-self___, Carry his cross and fol-low me

fol-low me ___ .

Theme 2
Theme Song: The Big Top

Words & music by John Hardwick

Verse 2:
Performers learn to trust and train
We can learn to do the same
Teamwork is the only way
They all have a part to play
The trapeze flies through the air
The Catcher always is right there
His timing's perfect there's no doubt
If we're late then we'll miss out!!

Action Song: God's People

Words & music by John Hardwick

God's people aren't super brave super he-roes, They don't have muscles from their heads to their toes, They're not gladi - a -tors, that's easy to see, In fact it's a-mazing - they are just like you and me! Sometimes scared Shaking & a-shiv'ring me!

God's

The Watt Family

Words & music by John Hardwick

But let's re- a-lise we're got God on our side And He can do abs-o-lute-ly an-y-thing! God's

meet the Watt fam' ly, meet the Watt fam' ly, a happy, wacky, crazy, ordin-ar-y fam-i-ly—. Meet the Watt fam' ly meet the Watt fam' ly, a loving, caring, sharing, ordin-a-ry fam-i-ly—.

152

I can do all things

Words & music by John Hardwick

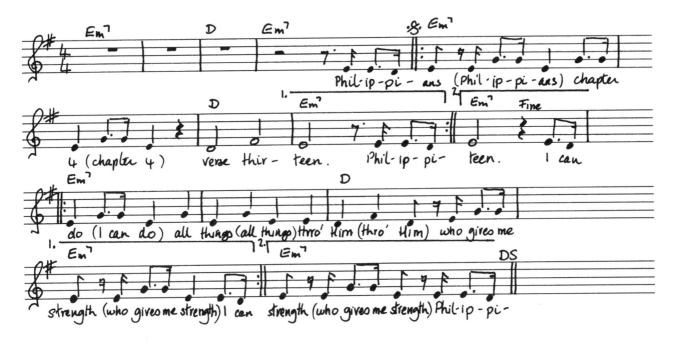

Phil-ip-pi-ans (Phil-ip-pi-ans) chapter 4 (chapter 4) verse thir-teen. Phil-ip-pi-teen. I can do (I can do) all things (all things) thro' Him (thro' Him) who gives me strength (who gives me strength) I can strength (who gives me strength) Phil-ip-pi-

Love of Christ

Words & music by John Hardwick

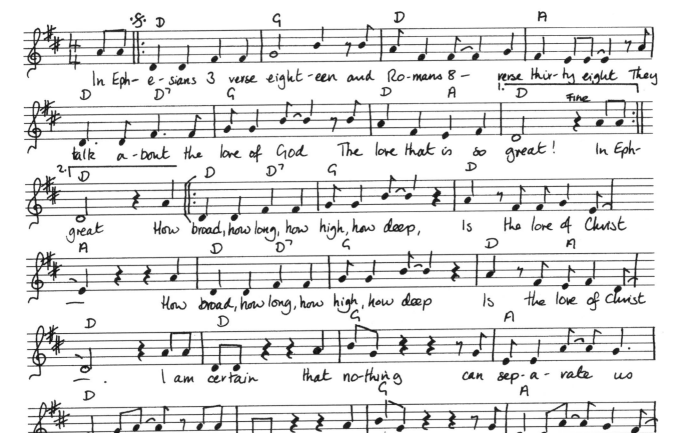

In Eph-e-sians 3 verse eight-een and Ro-mans 8-verse thir-ty eight They talk a-bout the love of God The love that is so great! In Eph-great How broad, how long, how high, how deep, Is the love of Christ How broad, how long, how high, how deep Is the love of Christ I am certain that no-thing can sep-a-rate us from His love, I am certain that nothing can sep-a-rate us from His love. How His love. In Eph-

My grace is sufficient for you

Words & music by John Hardwick

2 Cor-inth-i-ans, 12 verse 9; 2 Cor-
inth-i-ans 12 verse 9. My G. R. A. C. E.
is suf-fi-cient for you, My G. R. A. C. E.
is suf-fi-cient for you, For my power is made perfect in
weak — ness, Yes my power is made perfect in
weak — ness.

I have done my best

Words & music by John Hardwick

I have done my best in the race, I have run the full distance and
kept my faith, I have done my best in the race, 2
Timo-thy, chapter 4 verse se-ven. I have se-ven

154

I will always be with you (Matthew)

Words & music by John Hardwick

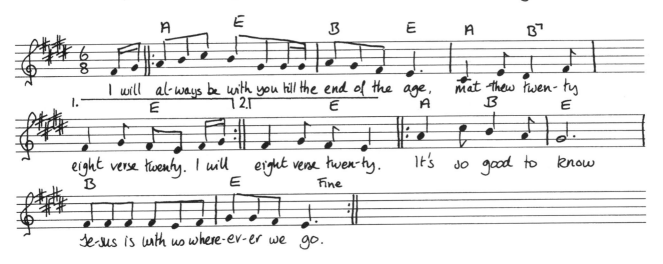

I will al-ways be with you till the end of the age, mat-thew twen-ty eight verse twenty. I will eight verse twen-ty. It's so good to know Je-sus is with us where-ev-er we go.

Theme 3

Theme Song:
Up there, out of this world

Words: Ruth Wills, Phil Brown, Paul Willmott
Music: Ruth Wills

Up there, out of this world, Rockets fly-ing high —
Up there, out of this world, stars go shooting by —. Up there,
out of this world, Gaz-ing up - a - bove — Up there, out of this world, God
made it out of love. 1. See moon & stars & a big black hole—, but
did you know who's in con-trol? God, He made them one by one,
cos His love, and His pow'r they go on and on — and on and

Verse 2:
Galaxies and nebulae
but ever stopped to wonder why.
God loves us, loves every one
coz his love and his pow'r
they go on and on and on and...

Choose yourself

Words & music by John Hardwick

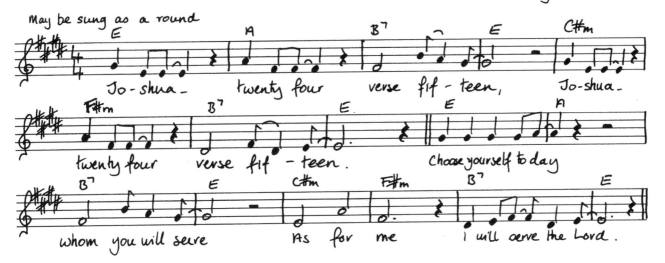

May be sung as a round

Jo-shua— twenty four verse fif - teen, Jo-shua— twenty four verse fif - teen. Choose yourself to day whom you will serve As for me I will serve the Lord.

Trust in the Lord

Words & music by John Hardwick

Trust in the Lord with all your heart & lean not on your own under-standing, Trust in the Lord with all your heart & lean not on your own under-standing. This is what it says in Pro-verbs 3 verse 5—. Don't re-ly on what you've got, learn to re-ly on the Lord!

Christll Jesus came

Words & music by John Hardwick

I will always be with you (Joshua)

Words & music by John Hardwick

We are on the victory side

Words & music by John Hardwick

Sometimes we are troubled — but not crushed, Sometimes we're in doubt —, but ne-ver in des-pair. There are many en-emies — but we al-ways have a friend, Al-though badly hurt at times, We are not des-troyed. We are on the vic-try side, God has won, Don't be fooled by Sa-tan's lies, God has won. We are on the vic-try side, God has won, We have got to re-a-lise God has, God has, God has, God has won!

2 Corinth-i-ans 4, verse 8 and 9.

THE ULTIMATE HOLIDAY CLUB
CASSETTE

A cassette featuring the songs, themes and memory verses from *The Ultimate Holiday Club Guide* is available from your local Christian bookshop, or, in case of difficulty, directly from BRF, price £5.99.

The Bible Reading Fellowship is a Registered Charity.

**The Bible Reading Fellowship,
Peter's Way, Sandy Lane West,
Oxford OX4 5HG**

Text copyright © John Hardwick and Alan Charter 1996

Illustrations copyright © Berni Georges 1996

The authors assert the moral right to be
identified as the authors of this work.

Published by
The Bible Reading Fellowship
Peter's Way, Sandy Lane West
Oxford OX4 5HG
ISBN 0 7459 3286 X
Albatross Books Pty Ltd
PO Box 320, Sutherland
NSW 2232, Australia
ISBN 0 7324 0948 9

First edition 1996
10 9 8 7 6 5 4 3 2 1 0

Acknowledgments
Unless otherwise stated, scripture is taken from the
Good News Bible published by The Bible
Societies/HarperCollins Publishers Ltd., UK, ©
American Bible Society, 1966, 1971, 1976, 1992

A catalogue record for this book is
available from the British Library

Printed and bound in Malta
by Interprint Limited